MW01616561

The Bible's Two Big Bangs

by

Richard L. "Dick" Ogden

BLACK FOREST PRESS
San Diego, California
March, 1997
First Edition

The Bible's Two Big Bangs

by

Richard L. "Dick" Ogden

PUBLISHED IN THE UNITED STATES OF AMERICA

BY

BLACK FOREST PRESS

539 TELEGRAPH CANYON ROAD BOX 521

CHULA VISTA, CA 91910

(619) 656-8048

Cover Design by Jan Lowry

Disclaimer

This document is an original work of the author. It may include reference to information commonly known or freely available to the general public. Any resemblance to other published information is purely coincidental. The author has in no way attempted to use material not of his own origination. Black Forest Press disclaims any association with or responsibility for the ideas, opinions or facts as expressed by the author of this book.

Printed in the United States of America
Library of Congress
Cataloging-in-Publication

ISBN: 1-881116-85-9

I wish to dedicate this book to my all time favorite Sunday School Class — the Hilltoppers (Senior Citizens) of the Rimrock Evangelical Free Church near Rapid City, South Dakota. It was their keen interest in prophetic subjects which motivated me to write this book.

𝔓reface

With the Rapture getting closer by the day and events in the Middle East and Europe taking place with accelerating speed, I have yielded to a relentless compulsion to write an exposé on the four major players in the Tribulation whom I believe are alive and ready right now to play out their roles in the upcoming world trauma that will soon plunge the planet into its worst ever nightmare.

I am continually frustrated by the never ending confusion there seems to be among writers on prophetic subjects, over which one of the beasts of Revelation 13 is the Antichrist. To miss the boat on that identification skews the interpretation one gives on just who does what, where and when in the Tribulation that rocks the world.

I'll leave it to others to focus on the blood and gore of the Tribulation along with its more sensational aspects. I'd like to limit this to an expose on the four major players in the tribulation and some of their more significant activities.

Table of Contents

Chapter

Introduction

The Tribulation *begins* with a big bang! — the Lord's *shout* as He comes for His own at the Rapture of the Church, the Body of Christ. He will catch them all up in the air in the twinkling of an eye — the living and the dead — to be forever with Him in heaven.

The voice of an archangel and the trumpet of God will add to His shout to make it one of the Bible's Big Bangs, and it won't have a thing to do with how the earth came into being, but will have everything to do with the wind-down of this earth as we have known it.

Those left behind on earth, all unbelievers, may very well hear an inarticulate sound like those who were with Saul of Tarsus at his conversion, when the Lord spoke to him, Acts 9:4-7. The world will be in turmoil, and won't know what to make of it all until the Roman ruler of the Revived Roman Empire gives his explanation for the sound that was heard and the mass exodus from this earth that takes place at the same instant.

A common theory is that the world will be so conditioned, as it is even now, by the supposed existence of UFO's — most probably a demonic phenomenon the devil has created for this very purpose — that the Roman ruler will announce that UFO's came and snatched all those people away to another planet and the noise that was heard was that of their departure. Further details as to this speculation will be included in comments on Revelation 13:6 in the upcoming chapter on Revelation 13.

The bang that *ends* the Tribulation will be the sound of *"the stone cut out without hands"* smiting the image of Daniel 2:34 upon its feet. That is part of the dream Daniel was given of the Messiah rudely terminating the existence of the Revived Roman Empire at the end of the Tribulation. This will include what He does at Armageddon to the armies of the world gathered in Israel to oppose Him.

This book is an attempt to properly identify four of the major players in the Tribulation; the false prophet as the Antichrist, who is the second Beast of Revelation 13; the first Beast of that same chapter who is the ruler of the Revived Roman Empire; the third major player will be the king of the north, the ruler of Russia; and the fourth major player is God, Himself — the Lord Jesus Christ, King of Kings and Lord of Lords. We will see His activities throughout the Tribulation, in addition.

This is also an attempt to explain how certain prophetic passages fit together to give us a credible scenario of some of the most significant events of the Tribulation that would seem to be approaching with amazing speed.

The following is a list of some of the intriguing questions that inevitably arise when one starts reading the passages of Scripture that are covered in the 7 chapters of this book:

- Will the Antichrist be a Jew or a Gentile?
  - Will the church go through the tribulation?
- Who are the two Beasts of Revelation 13?
  - Who are the members of the unholy trinity?
- How do we get from the present 12 nations in the Common Market to the Biblical 10 in the Tribulation?
  - When will Israel be invaded and Armageddon take place?
- What is the mark of the Beast?

All of these questions, and more, will be dealt with in the ensuing chapters. All Scriptures quoted are in the *King James Version* unless otherwise indicated.

Chapter One

2 Thessalonians 2:1-12 is a most strategic chapter in this book about future prophetic events because it not only speaks of the sudden appearance on the world scene of the Antichrist, but also because it gives us an important clue as to the identity of the man of sin (verse 3), that lawless one (*"wicked one"* in the KJV, verse 8), the son of perdition (verse 3) who is the Antichrist.

The clue is the statement in verse 4 that *he sits in the temple of God, showing himself that he is God.* Of the two prime candidates for the dubious distinction of being the Antichrist, the *second* Beast of Revelation 13:11-18, lines up with this statement best.

The second Beast, the false prophet (Revelation 19:20), is the one who presents himself to Israel as the Messiah. He is antichrist in *both* meanings of the Greek word anti. He is *in place of* as well as *against* the Messiah. He is Satan's counterfeit of the true Messiah, the Lord Jesus Christ. The other prime candidate for being the Antichrist is the first Beast of Revelation 13:1-10, the leader of the Revived Roman Empire, a worldwide dictator, yet he is merely *against* the true Messiah, but *not in place of Him.*

As a counterfeit of the true Messiah, the *false prophet* will also be a priest as well as a prophet and king, just as Jesus is. And as a priest, he will be able to sit in the temple as God, yet in reality he will oppose God and exalt himself above all that is called God or that is worshipped (verse 4). The reason he will oppose God is because his coming will be after the working of Satan, as verse 9 says. Only a *Jew* will be able to fulfill the role of the Messiah, true Messiah *or* false. Therefore, the second Beast, the false prophet, will have to be a Jew. But the first Beast will in all probability be a *Gentile* and rule a world of largely made up of Gentiles.

Another name commonly attributed to the Antichrist, i.e., the second Beast, is *the willful king* of Daniel 11:36. This verse also depicts him as exalting himself, magnifying himself above every god and speaking marvelous (blasphemous) things against the God of gods. Verse 37 of Daniel 11 alludes to his identity as the false prophet in that he does not regard the desire of women. All women of the tribe of Judah hoped to be the mother of the Messiah.

The apostle John warned his readers *"that antichrist shall come,"* 1 John 2:18. In his gospel he warned of *"an hireling shepherd"* who leaves the sheep and flees so that the wolf can scatter the sheep, but the good Shepherd lays down His life for the sheep, John 10:12-15. This hireling shepherd can only refer to the false prophet as the Antichrist. Even though this is not a prophetic context, the next one in Zechariah is prophetic.

Zechariah referred to the same shepherd as the *worthless shepherd* who leaves the flock, Zechariah 11:17. The Antichrist will evidently flee the land of Palestine when Israel is invaded by the south, north, east and west, just as John says of *the hireling shepherd* in John 10:12-15. What a contrast to our Good Shepherd, Who willingly endured such a horrendous death for His sheep, and Who will never, never forsake us! (Hebrews 13:5).

Now, let us work our way through this enlightening passage and explore carefully and slowly the rise and fall of the second Beast, the Antichrist.

The Rise and Fall of the Second Beast — The Antichrist — 2 Thessalonians 2:1-12

The first three verses speak of *the Rapture of the Church and then the almost immediate revelation of the Antichrist.*

*"Now we beseech you, brethren, by the coming of our
Lord Jesus Christ, and by our gathering together unto
him, that ye be not soon shaken in mind, or be troubled,
neither by spirit, nor by word, nor by letter as from us,
as that the day of the Lord is present. Let no man
deceive you by any means; for that day shall not come,
except there come the falling away first, and that man
of sin be revealed, the son of perdition."*

It is with reference to ("by") the coming of our Lord Jesus
Christ that Paul *"beseeches"* or requests his readers to not soon be
shaken. And to make sure which coming he meant to specify, he
referred to the Rapture by saying, *"namely by our gathering
together unto him."* The English translation here is *"and"*, but
what kind of "and" is it — sequential or explanatory? I believe
the context would insist on the *explanatory* use of "and", thus the
word *namely* is what should be used here.

The Thessalonian believers were shaking in their boots
because they thought the Rapture had taken place and that they
were actually in the Tribulation. They were evidently told that
"by word" from some false teachers, as well as by a forged
"letter" (3:17), purported to be from Paul, teaching that *"the day
of the Lord is present."*

The *"day of the Lord"* refers to times in human history when
the Lord chooses to intervene and bless His people or punish His
enemies. Nebuchadnezzar's defeat of Pharaoh-Necho's Egypt is
an example of *vengeance* on His adversaries where the term "day
of the Lord" is used of an event in Old Testament times, Jeremiah
46:10-11. As for an event in New Testament times, the choices
are many where the term "day of the Lord" is used.

We know that term, or its equivalent, is used more than 200
times by the prophets of old. Zechariah 14:1-21 uses the term to
refer to the destruction of the armies of the world at Armageddon,
so we see it used of a past and a future event. But, in this par-
ticular future event we also are able to see the *blessing* of God's
people in that the Lord will rule in His Millennial Kingdom with
peace, justice and prosperity for all who are in it.

In verse 2, in this passage, we will actually see the term used in
both of its meanings. The Rapture will be *blessing* on His Church,
and the revelation of the man of sin, the Antichrist, just after the
Rapture, will refer to the *punishing* of Christ-rejecters in the

Tribulation by way of the Antichrist and his policies, plus the judgments of the Tribulation itself.

Paul did not want the Thessalonians to be deceived by any means — by unexplained miracles, intellectual means or emotional means — as to that day of the Lord. His big point, in verse 3, is that they cannot be in that day — the Tribulation — until the *"falling away"* takes place first.

The falling away is the Greek word "apostasia," which usually refers to the departure from the faith that we associate with the word apostasy. But this departure, according to the very clear context of verse one of *"our gathering together unto him"*, is the departure of the Church from this world at the Rapture when *"the Lord himself shall descend from heaven with a shout, with the voice of the archangel, and with the trump of God; and the dead in Christ shall rise first; then we who are alive and remain shall be caught up together with them in the clouds, to meet the Lord in the air; and so shall we ever be with the Lord."* 1 **Thessalonians 4: 17-18**. In fact, Wycliff translated the word "apostasia", in verse three, as *"our gathering unto Him"*. Other interpreters like Dwight Pentecost view this the same way — the Rapture of the Church.

The next important key word comes two verses later in the word *"and"*, only this time it is not an explanatory "and" but is a sequential "and". These are best translated "and then" to denote sequence of movement.

This means that the Rapture takes place first — removing the Church from this earth — and very soon thereafter *"that man of sin ... the son of perdition"* (the Antichrist) will be revealed. The word for "sin" in this descriptive phrase for the Antichrist, is not the usual word for sin, but is the word for *lawless*. That same word is used in verse 8 in describing him as *"that wicked one"*. So, he literally is both the *"man of lawlessness"* and *"that lawless one"* that is revealed here in this chapter.

The name *"son of perdition"* refers to the eternal destiny of the Antichrist — destruction in a lake of fire, just as Revelation 19:20 speaks of him at the end of the Tribulation — being *"cast alive into a lake of fire burning with brimstone"*. Jesus referred to Judas as the *"son of perdition"* in John 17:12, and he had the same eternal destiny as the Antichrist will have and all unbelievers, for that matter, who leave this earth without having trusted in Christ as Savior. It is interesting to note that both Judas and the Antichrist pretend to be true believers.

Verses 4-5 show the Antichrist claiming to be God.

"Who opposeth and exalteth himself above all that is called God, or that is worshipped, so that he, as God, sitteth in the temple of God, showing himself that he is God. (5) Remember ye not that, when I was with you, I told you these things?"

Verse 4 reveals just how anti or *against* God that he is in addition to being anti in the sense of *in place of* God. He *opposes* God and *exalts himself above God or anything that is worshipped* because he is like the one who empowers him — Satan. When Lucifer, just before he fell and became Satan, was in heaven as *"the anointed cherub"*, Ezekiel 28:14 - the personal attendant of Christ - he said, *"I will ascend into heaven, I will exalt my throne above the stars of God...I will be like the Most High,"* **Isaiah 14:13-14.**

As to worship, he wants it, but he won't mind sharing it evidently, for in Revelation 13:14-15 he has his people, the Jews in Israel, make an image of the first Beast that all might worship it. And in Daniel 11:38 he shall honor the god of fortresses. As will be pointed out, in Chapter Four of this book, on Daniel 11, it would appear that the Antichrist will, at first, recognize no other god but himself - thinking that he himself is god - but will change his mind a little later on in order to placate and cooperate with the first Beast for reasons that will be explained more fully there.

He will, however, be qualified to *"sit in the temple, showing himself that he is God"* because he will either be able to fake his credentials *as a priest*, or can actually trace his lineage to the tribe of Levi. Furthermore, he can sit there *as the Messiah*, which he falsely claims to be.

When Paul was with the Thessalonians in person, he reminds them in this letter that he told them, no doubt, about *"the willful king"* of Daniel 11:36 who is the same person he is now writing about. But he dares not mention him by that name in writing for fear that it would be used against them as treason, just as happened to Jason in the book of Acts where he was accused of doing things *"contrary to the decrees of Caesar, saying that there is another king, one Jesus."* **Acts 17:7.**

Verse 6 tells us of the restraining ministry of the Holy Spirit on Satan before the Tribulation.

"And now ye know what restraineth that he might be revealed in his time."

Paul seems to be assuming that they already know about the Holy Spirit's restraining ministry, probably because he told them in person when he was with them.

"What" restrains is in the neuter gender probably to focus on the *power* of the Holy Spirit rather than His person at this point. In verse 7 the *person* of God is meant when the masculine gender is used for *"he"* who now hinders.

The Holy Spirit restrains Satan in the world, especially now when the Rapture is nearer than ever, so that the Antichrist won't be prematurely revealed in order that he *"might be revealed in his time"*. His time is during these end times of the 70th week of Daniel, the time of Jacob's trouble, - i.e., the Tribulation. Satan has always had a man ready in case God said "Now is the time".

Verse 7 speaks of Satan's activity as the mystery of iniquity.

"For the mystery of iniquity doth already work, only he who now hindereth will continue to hinder until he be taken out of the way."

The mystery is that Satan operates in this church age in his iniquitous ways and has been doing so (*"doth already work"*) throughout the church age. The Holy Spirit will do this restraining until "he", the Holy Spirit, is taken out of the way. He is not completely removed from this world, but His restraint on Satan is removed. Satan will then, after the Rapture, be free to reveal his man, the Antichrist, even as verse 8 says.

While the context limits the restraint in this passage to Satan, yet it is still true that the Holy Spirit does restrain evil in the world today, and without that restraint the world would be what it will be in the Tribulation - the world gone mad on a sin binge. Even in the Tribulation the Holy Spirit will remain in the world in the lives of Tribulation believers and will be enabling them. Even at that, without morality the human race cannot long survive.

Verse 8 describes, the rise and demise of the Antichrist.

"And then shall that wicked one be revealed, whom the Lord shall consume with the spirit of his mouth, and shall destroy with the brightness of his coming."

"Then" is best taken as a demonstrative adverb of time: as W.E. Vine, in his *Expository Dictionary of New Testament Words*, puts it. This word gives a dramatic suddenness to the sequence of the Rapture being almost immediately followed by *that lawless one* taking center stage as Satan reveals him to the world. As pointed out in verse 7, *"wicked"* is the same word for *"iniquity"* and means *lawless*. This is all it says in this verse about the *rise* of the Antichrist. But that rise is covered more extensively in Revelation 13:11, on which we will comment in the next chapter.

Now as to his *demise*, we're told here that the Lord shall consume him. This means that he'll be destroyed with the breath of the Lord's mouth. **Revelation 19:15** gives us that picture where it says, *"and out of his mouth goeth a sharp sword, that with it he should smite the nations"*. This refers to God's spoken word. It is the same spoken word of His that He used in creating this universe. He just spoke it into existence. **Isaiah 11:4** says *"and he shall smite the earth with the rod of his mouth, and with the breath of his lips shall he slay the wicked."*

It looks like He'll also use the radiance of His appearance at His second coming to destroy him. **Matthew 24:27** says of that coming, *"For as the lightning cometh out of the east, and shineth even unto the west, so shall also the coming of the Son of man be."* Verse 30 adds that *"then shall all the tribes of the earth mourn, and they shall see the Son of man coming in the clouds of heaven with power and great glory."*

We know from **Revelation 19:20** that his destruction will be accomplished by their being *"cast alive into a lake of fire burning with brimstone (21) And the remnant were slain with the sword of him that sat upon the horse, which sword proceeded out of his mouth."* All that, of course, happens at the end of the Tribulation after the returning King of Kings and Lord of Lords disposes of the armies of the world that have united to fight against Him at the battle of Armageddon.

Verses 9-10 speak of the power of the Antichrist and his deceptions.

> *"Even him whose coming is after the working of Satan with all power and signs and lying wonders, (10) And with all deceivableness of unrighteousness in them that perish, because they received not the love of the truth, that they might be saved."*

It is the Antichrist whose *"coming"*, or appearance, is in accordance with the working of Satan. He will be indwelt by a powerful demon from the beginning of the Tribulation through the end of it. The first Beast, as we will see in Chapter Two of this book, will be indwelt by a demon in the first half of the Tribulation, but by Satan personally in the last half.

The Antichrist will have *"all"* or *every* kind of miracle power, like giving life to the image of the beast as it says in Revelation 13:15. That's one example of it. *"Signs"*, here in verse 9, will be the type of miracle designed to convey a certain message. The message he will want to convey is that *he is God* and has divine supernatural power. Yet his *"signs"* will never equal the supernatural power displayed by the Holy Spirit in His miracles.

The *"lying"* or deceiving *"wonders"* are miracles to inspire *awe* that he has supernatural power, like fire coming down from heaven on earth in the sight of men just as Revelation 13:13 says.

The *"deceivableness of unrighteousness"* of verse 10 means that everything the Antichrist does is unrighteous. **2 Corinthians 4:4** sheds light on this: *"In whom the god of this age hath blinded the minds of them who believe not, lest the light of the glorious gospel of Christ, who is the image of God, should shine unto them."* Satan loves to blind men, women, boys and girls any old way he can, and as the father of lies and as an angel of light (2 Corinthians 11:14), he is the master of deception, and so are his servants — Beasts one and two.

Verses 11-12 speak of strong delusion, the lie and pleasure in unrighteousness.

> *"And for this cause God shall send them strong delusion, that they should believe the lie, (12) That they all might be judged who believed not the truth, but had pleasure in unrighteousness."*

What is *this cause* that caused God to send the unbelievers of the Tribulation *"strong delusion"*? It would seem to be a special one time only judicial blindness to those who had heard the Gospel prior to the Rapture, had rejected it and had the idea that they could change their minds later on, such as after the Rapture. Those who had not heard the Gospel prior to the Rapture and are now alive during the Tribulation will not have that strong delusion. Romans 11:25 gives an example of such judicial blindness imposed by God on the Jews in Jesus'day.

"The lie" that the deluded *"should believe"* is probably that the Antichrist is God. Multitudes will believe that and will, therefore, receive the mark of the Beast of Revelation 13:16-17 as an indication of that belief and as evidence of their *submission* to the first Beast of Revelation 13 and his system, and their worship of him. Failure to receive that mark may result in death, torture, hunger, privation and/or fugitive status because there will be no buying or selling without the mark.

Verse 12 gives the *final statement about all who might be judged*. They are people who *"believed not the truth"*. When a person believes in the truth about the deity and work of Christ on the cross for him or her, he or she passes from spiritual death to spiritual life and thereby removes himself or herself from this category of people being judged, **John 3:36:** *"He that believeth on the Son hath everlasting life; and he that believeth not the Son shall not see life, but the wrath of God abideth on him."*

The judged ones are also those who *"had pleasure in unrighteousness"*. We are told that there is a certain *stimu - lation* attached to belief in the falsehood of unrighteousness akin to ecstasy. The *"unrighteousness"* is the *falsehood* of religion which is the opposite of the truth because religion is do, do, do, in order to be saved, while true Christianity is *done*: Christ did all the work on the cross for salvation, and there is nothing left to be done. "It is finished" just as Christ cried out on the cross. Christianity is a personal belief in Christ and a relationship to that crucified and resurrected One.

Chapter Two

Revelation 13 is a fascinating chapter for several reasons: it identifies two of the major players in the Tribulation as the first Beast and the second Beast, as well as the empire that the first Beast rules. It also reveals the character of these two men, their power source and some of the evil and deceitful things they do.

One of the things the second Beast does is to make a statue image of the first Beast as well as the mark of the first Beast which all must wear in their right hand or on their foreheads. Without this mark they will be unable to buy or sell, thus putting their very survival at extreme risk.

Let's now work our way, verse by verse and symbol by symbol, through this strange chapter which outlines the rise and fall of the first Beast in the Tribulation - the ruler of the Revived Roman Empire. Then we'll see the rise of the second Beast, the dictator of Israel, the false prophet who is the Antichrist. The fascinating part will be the details we'll be able to pick up as we carefully proceed examining these 18 verses. For the fall of the second Beast, the Antichrist, we need to refer to Chapter One concerning 2 Thessalonians 2:8.

The Rise and Fall of the First Beast, Revelation 13:1-10.

The first three verses speak of *the political empire of this beast as depicted in the first half of the Tribulation.*

> *"And I stood upon the sand of the sea, and saw a beast rise up out of the sea, having seven heads and ten horns, and upon his horns ten crowns, and upon his heads the name of blasphemy. (2) And the beast which I saw was like a leopard, and his feet were like the feet of a bear, and his mouth like the mouth of a lion; and the dragon gave him his power, and his throne and great authority. (3) And I saw one of his heads as though it were wounded to death; and his deadly wound was healed, and all the world wondered after the beast."*

The Beast that John saw in *verse 1*, represents the Revived Roman Empire as it arises out of the sea of nations. The emphasis will shift, in verse 4, to the *person* who heads up that empire, and he too will be called a Beast.

This empire is called a Beast because it is part of a group of nations - seven in all - that dominated Israel militarily and politically at one time or another in its history. Starting with Egypt, they included Assyria, Babylonia, Persia, Greece, Rome and lastly the Revived Roman Empire. They are referred to, in verse 1, as *"seven heads"* on the beast. Chapter 12, verse 3 also refers to those same heads.

Verse 2 of Chapter 13 describes this empire in terms of a beast similar to the three wild beasts with whom we all are familiar.

The leopard refers to the military *speed* of this Revived Roman Empire just as it did for the leopard in Daniel 7 in Daniel's description of Greece. The bear speaks of military *strength* even as it did for Persia in Daniel 7. The lion represents *ferocity* just as with the Babylonian Empire in Daniel 7. The Revived Roman Empire of the Tribulation will have all three of these going for it as well, as will its ruler, Beast number one, personally. He will move quickly and be strong and fierce.

As for *power* given to the first Beast, it will be Satan, who is called *"the dragon"*, here in verse 2, who gives it to him. Its power and authority will come from one of Satan's demons in the first half of the Tribulation. Then, in the middle of the Tribulation, when Satan is cast down to this earth, as 12:8 says, Satan himself will move in and replace the demon and personally will indwell the first Beast. He can only indwell one person at a time, so this is the one - the ruler of the Revived Roman Empire!

Daniel also speaks of *"the sea"* (7:3) and he too meant the sea of gentile nations. In John's case, he saw a single beast rather than four rise up out of the sea. All this would seem to indicate that the first Beast of Revelation 13 is a *Gentile*, while the second Beast of that chapter is a *Jew* because he presents himself to Israel as their Messiah, even as Daniel 11:36-37 seems to indicate. (See Chapter Four of this book for details on the passage.)

The first beast, as the Revived Roman Empire, has as its core 10 independent nations, *"the 10 horns"* of 13:1 and 12:3. These will probably be independent democracies which will have surrendered their sovereignty to the first Beast who will rule as dictator over them in the first half of the Tribulation, but by the second half he'll be a world dictator.

Dr. Charles R. Taylor, who has a prophetic radio ministry, wrote a book titled *The Antichrist King - Juan Carlos*. In it he develops a very likely scenario in which he not only makes a compelling case for Juan Carlos, presently King of Spain, as the one who will shortly rule the world as the first Beast, but also identifies the 10 nations.

At the present time, he says there are 12 nations in the EEC– the European Economic Community. Austria has her application in to become number 13, and he indicates that it is only a matter of time — like a year or two — and she'll be in since there appears to be no opposition. With the elimination of three of the present 12, that leaves 10 after the start of the Tribulation with Austria on board. If Austria were approved before the Rapture, the elimination of the three nations would still leave 10 after the Rapture.

Daniel speaks of these three horns as *"plucked up by the roots"* by the *"little horn"* of 7:8. The little horn is the end time leader of the Revived Roman Empire, the Roman Prince of 9:26-27, namely the first Beast of Revelation 13. Taylor identified the three nations as Ireland, Greece and Denmark - all three of them too pacifistic for such an aggressive and adventuristic dictator.

These *"10 horns"* of verse 1 are the same 10 nations as the 10 *"toes"* of Daniel 2:41-42. But the *"10 crowns"* speak of *political power* and refer to the fact that they go into the Tribulation as independent nations, even democracies.

"The names of blasphemy" upon his heads would seem to indicate that bad mouthing God is the glue that binds them all together - something they have in common.

Verse 3 of Chapter 13 uses language which depicts the fall of the Roman Empire and the revival of same.

The old Roman Empire is referred to as a head being *"wounded to death"*, and it was one of the seven heads, or nations, that dominated Israel militarily and politically at one time in its history. This wound occurred in 476 A.D. when Emperor Romulus Augustus was taken captive by the German barbarians thus ending the line of the Roman Emperors. But the *"deadly wound was healed"* refers to the revival of that empire during the first half of the Tribulation.

Verses 4-8 show the first Beast as a person instead of as an empire, as did verses 1-3.

Empires - especially dictatorships - are usually led by a person, and this will be no exception; that and his religious activity will be the emphasis in these verses.

"And they worshipped the dragon who gave power unto the beast; and they worshipped the beast, saying, Who is like the beast? Who is able to make war with him? (5) And there was given unto him a mouth speaking great things and blasphemies, and power was given unto him to continue forty and two months. (6) And he opened his mouth in blasphemy against God, to blaspheme his name, and his tabernacle, and them that dwell in heaven. (7) And it was given unto him to make war with the saints, and to overcome them; and power was given him over all kindreds, and tongues and nations. (8) And all that dwell upon the earth shall worship him, whose names are not written in the book of life of the Lamb slain from the foundation of the world."

To worship Satan's man is to worship Satan, who in verse 4 is called *"the dragon"*, one of his many names. He empowers the *person*, who leads the Revived Roman Empire, as the Beast who receives worship and who questions whether there is anybody like him and whether anyone is able to make war with him. Chapter 6 verse 2 shows him as the rider on a white horse going forth *"conquering, and to conquer"*. Roman emperors rode white horses, by the way.

As to being worshipped, both he and the false prophet receive worship, which fits right in with the unholy trinity, the Satanic counterfeit of the true Trinity. The Roman leader best represents the Father; the false prophet, the Antichrist, represents the Son; while the Holy Spirit is best represented by Satan who performs miracles by his own supernatural power.

Verse 5 speaks of the Beast's eloquent public speaking ability.

Daniel 7:8 says he'll have *"a mouth speaking great things"*. He'll evidently be exceptionally eloquent, and, as verse 6 says in Revelation 13, he'll speak blasphemies, the specifics of which we will see in verse 6.

The *"power"* that will be given him to continue three and one half years (42 months) would seem to suggest the probability that Satan will have indwelt him for the last half of the Tribulation when his power will be at its peak. In the first half, he will probably be demon possessed; then, when Satan is cast out of heaven to the earth (12:10), he'll choose to indwell this first Beast and cause him to be a worldwide dictator.

Verse 6 gives us the blasphemous eloquence of the first Beast.

When a demon or Satan possesses a person, the eloquence should not be surprising, for such ability emanates from the supernatural. Nor should one wonder about the blasphemies, for the same reason, when the source is considered.

The *"blasphemies against God and His name"* may well be attacks against the Church as well as God because of a couple of clues that immediately follow that statement. All Christians are members of the Body of Christ, the Church, both individually and corporately. Such members are also referred to as the temple of God (1 Corinthians 3:16) which is also a reference to the "tabernacle" of God which was replaced by the temple of God. At that point in time the Church is in heaven, thus we have the phrase used here of the Church, *"them that dwell in heaven"*.

With those clues, coupled with the Church in heaven which they point to, we assume that this Roman Ruler of the Revived Roman Empire will find it necessary to try to explain away the sudden mass exodus of multiplied millions of Christians which is known in Christendom as the Rapture. We also assume that he succeeds in doing so because otherwise it would greatly interfere with his program of world domination. The intriguing part, though, is what his explanation will be. As the eloquent one he is, and energized by Satan, the father of lies, he undoubtedly makes a credible case such as the possibility of the one that is popular today. UFOs came down and took them all away since they were the real bad cells in the true cosmic world order and were removed by the power of the Beast. New Agers today try to depict true Christians as the bad guys who are gumming up the works and are opposed to the new world order.

To show how conditioned we are getting, NPR commentator Andrei Codrescu said, on radio December 19, 1995, commenting on the Rapture passage, **1 Thessalonians 4:17**, "The evaporation of four million [people] who believe in this crap would leave the world an instantly better place."

Verse 7 indicates that the first Beast will have worldwide power.

He will be permitted by God *"to make war"* with believers of the Tribulation *"and to overcome them"* through death. The Tribulation will prove to be the greatest period of martyrdom in history (6:9-11; 7:9-14; 12:17), but also of evangelism, as well (7:4-8; 10:3-9; 14:6-7). The impact then of believers dying with fearlessness and courage born of dying grace will be of the kind the first century is noted for, but on a larger scale.

In verse 8 we see that he also will be worshipped worldwide.

He will be worshipped only by unbelievers, for that is the status of all *"whose names are not written in the book of life"*. Everyone born into the human race has his name written in the book of life because when Christ died on the cross, He rendered the entire human race savable. One is blotted out of the book when one is no longer savable, at the end of physical life on earth without having trusted in Christ as Savior. It is the *Lamb's* book, for He is the Lamb of God who takes away the sins of the world, John 1:29.

The book was written from before "the foundation of the world". Foundation of the world goes with the book of life and not with the Lamb slain. The Lamb was not slain before the foundation of the world even though it was planned before that.

Verses 9 and 10 invite believers in the Tribulation to hang tough.

> *"If any man have an ear, let him hear. (10) He that leadeth into captivity shall go into captivity; he that killeth with the sword must be killed with the sword. Here is the patience and the faith of the saints."*

The invitation is in verse 9 *"to hear"*, while the hanging tough is in the words *"Here is the patience and the faith of the saints"* in verse 10.

There are some significant words missing from verse 9 that appeared with the phrase above about having an ear to hear in 2:7, 11, 17, 29; 3:6, 13 and 22 when John was talking about the seven churches on earth when he wrote this book. *"What the Spirit saith unto the churches"* is missing in 13:9 because the Church was caught up to heaven at the Rapture. It is not on the earth during the Tribulation — just one more of the many bits of evidence that exist in the Bible for the pre-Tribulation Rapture position.

Also taught in verse 10 is the principle that is also in **Romans 12:19** where it says *"Vengeance is mine, I will repay saith the Lord"*, i.e., when anyone captures or kills a child of God, the Lord will see that justice is meted out sooner or later.

In the case of the first Beast, he will be *"killed with the sword"* (symbolic of death here) for inflicting death upon believers in Christ during the Tribulation. Death and enslavement for the first Beast will be when Satan and the two Beasts will be incarcerated in the abyss for the 1,000 years of the Millennium, and then after that in the lake of fire for all eternity, Revelation 19:20-21.

Verses 14-19 of that chapter describe the armies of this world being killed with the sharp sword of the mouth of the King of Kings and Lord of Lords. This will happen when Christ returns at His second coming to make war against the Beast and the kings of the earth and their armies. Both the captivity and the killing with the sword are cases of poetic justice being rendered — both in keeping with **Romans 12:19**, *"Vengeance is mine, I will repay, saith the Lord"*. This principle holds true for every child of God that is martyred in human history. God deals with it in His own time.

The Rise, Activities and Fall of the Second Beast, Revelation 13:11-18; 19:20; 20:10

The fall of this Beast is stated in 19:20; 20:10 and 2 Thessalonians 2:8 (see Chapter 1 of this book). He, as well as the first Beast, ends up in the lake of fire.

This second Beast will also be controlled by Satan, but through demon possession, for Satan can only possess one person at a time since he is not omnipresent. He'll save that personal indwelling for the first Beast in the middle of the Tribulation when he is cast out of heaven to this earth, 12:10. The second Beast will be allied with the first Beast, the Roman dictator, to the extent of a peace and trade agreement even to the promoting of the worship of the first Beast, as the details in this passage will reveal.

This false prophet has many aliases — *the willful king, that wicked one, the son of perdition, the man of sin, an hireling shepherd the worthless shepherd,* and *the Antichrist,* all of which were documented in Chapter One of this book.

Verse 11 describes the rise of this second Beast.

> *"And I beheld another beast coming up out of the earth; and he had two horns like a lamb, and he spoke like a dragon."*

He, too, will be a dictator, but a Jew and not a Gentile as was the first Beast, thus he will be "another" (allos) of the same kind — that is, a dictator.

He will be from the *land* of Palestine for the word *"earth"* can also be translated land and best fits this context. He will present himself to the Jews in Israel and to the world as the Messiah. He will be *the Antichrist* in the sense of the word anti - *in place of* - Christ. Both Beasts will be antichrist in the other meaning of anti - against Christ. Beast number two is called the false prophet because Jesus, the true Messiah *was* a prophet.

The *first Beast* will be the political dictator of not only the Revived Roman Empire but the entire world by the middle of the Tribulation. He'll also be the ruler of the world's one ecumenical religion. The man he uses to head up that one-world church will be destroyed by him in the second half of the Tribulation, which will leave him in total control of it. Chapters 17 and 18 of Revelation deal with all that.

The *second Beast* will be the political and religious dictator of Israel employing *his* own interpretation of the Massic Law. And to sweeten the Daniel 9:27 peace treaty that the first Beast makes with Israel at the beginning of the Tribulation, he will make a certain trade agreement with the second Beast to strengthen the economic position of the second Beast (Daniel 11:38-39). In exchange for this, the second Beast will have his people put up a statue of the first Beast, (13:14) in the temple to be worshipped at the middle of the Tribulation.

The *"two horns like a lamb"* tell us a couple of things: he's a *male* and a *false Messiah*, for the true Messiah is known in scripture as the Lamb of God. He will fulfill the words of Jesus in **John 5:43**, *"I am come in my Father's name, and ye received me not; if another shall come in his own name, him ye will receive."*

The phrase *"he spoke like a dragon"* indicates he is controlled by Satan (the dragon) through possession by a demon.

Verse 12 alludes to the peace treaty that the first Beast makes with the second Beast and Israel.

> *"And he exerciseth all the power of the first beast before him, and causeth the earth and them who dwell on it to worship the first beast, whose deadly wound was healed."*

The allusion comes from the words *"before him"* in verse 12. The Greek word for *"before"* means *in the presence of* and refers to the meeting between the two Beasts where the first Beast makes a peace treaty with Israel guaranteeing them peace and safety in the land of Palestine. Then the first Beast will make the trade agreement with the second Beast. To enhance that, a little later on the second Beast agrees to have his people, the Jews, put up a statue of the first Beast to be worshipped. It is described in Matthew 24:15 as the abomination of desolation, but it does not happen until the middle of the Tribulation when **Daniel 9:27** says *"and in the midst of the week he shall cause the sacrifice and the oblation to cease"*.

When verse 12 says *"he exerciseth all the power of the first beast"*, it means the second beast rules with the same *authority* of the first Beast. They will both have *dictatorial* authority. The statue will be the mechanism that will cause the land of Israel to worship the first Beast. Later on in the last half of the Tribulation, the earth, in the sense of the *whole world*, will worship him. It will be, in essence, a replay of emperor worship as it was in the old Roman Empire.

"*Whose deadly wound was healed*", has the same meaning that we saw in verse 3 where it meant the *revival* of the old Roman Empire during the Tribulation.

Verse 13 gives us further insight into the nature of the second Beast.

> *"And he doeth great wonders, so that he maketh fire come down from heaven on the earth in the sight of men."*

Being demon possessed, he has power to do miracles of all kinds. (see also 16:13-14.) Such miracle powers are counterfeits of the power of the Holy Spirit. Revelation 16:13-14 is an example of Satan's counterfeit of the Holy Trinity and may aptly be called the unholy trinity, described in our comments on verses 4-8.

Verses 14-15 give us some fascinating details about the image of the Beast.

> *"And deceiveth them that dwell on the earth by the means of those miracles which he had power to do in the sight of the beast, saying to them that dwell on the earth, that they should make an image to the beast, that had the wound by a sword, and did live. (15) And he hath power to give life unto the image of the beast that the image of the beast should both speak, and cause that as many as would not worship the image of the beast should be killed."*

All will be deceived in the land of Israel by the statue and by the miracles (like fire from heaven) except those who heed the warnings in Daniel 11:41 and Matthew 24:15-20 and who flee to the hills and mountains of Edom, Moab and Ammon.

The first Beast, who had "*the wound by a sword and did live*", verse 14, is the same as in verse 12, "*the first beast whose deadly wound was healed*", and that goes back to verse 3 where it referred to the Revived Roman Empire. It is the first beast to be mentioned in Chapter 13.

The statue will not be some weird monster with seven heads, 10 horns and 10 crowns, as the beast of verse 1 is described. It will be a replica of the *person* of Beast number one (verse 4), the *person* who heads up the Revived Roman Empire.

The word for *"life"*, in verse 15, is not the usual word for it, which is *psuche*. Here it is *pneuma* which means breath, and no doubt was used to refer to the *speaking* ability of the statue.

There are a couple of credible possibilities for this phenomenon. Modern technology can make even a cash register speak, as most of us have already found out at the supermarket checkout counter. There are also robots that can speak because they are programmed to do so. They are very life-like in appearance. So the technology for this *"miracle"* is already avaible.

The second possibility is demons who can indwell the statue and throw their voices like a ventriloquist, as recorded in Isaiah 8:19 and Isaiah 29:4. It well might be that the latter will be employed due to the limited time in which to make such a talking statue and also due to the obvious demonic power that will be on the scene. In either case it will *appear* that the second Beast actually gives genuine life to the image of the Beast.

All who will not worship the image of the Beast will be killed, probably by fire that comes out of the mouth of the statue that the people will have made of the first Beast. The second Beast will have the power to make fire come down from heaven to earth (verse 13), so why could he not make fire come out of the mouth of a statue? And fire, by the way, will come out of the mouths of God's two witnesses in Revelation 11:5, and we must not forget that Satan is a master counterfeiter of almost everything that God does.

If fire is the way the executions will happen, it looks like they'll have to bring the rebels to the statue for it. Otherwise they could just hunt them down and shoot them or behead them (20:4) right on the spot where they are found.

In verses 16-17, we see that the mark of the Beast is part of the worldwide ecumenical religious system.

> *"And he causeth all, both small and great, rich and poor, free and enslaved, to receive a mark in their right hand, or in their foreheads, (17) And that no man might buy or sell, except he that had the mark, or the name of the beast, or the number of his name."*

You talk about pressure to join a religion; this is the ultimate! If they *won't* worship the image of the Beast, they'll be ostracized, starved, tortured or killed, as is the case in verse 15 where they are caught red–handed.

If they *do* worship it, they must also receive the mark of the Beast in their right hand or forehead. That determines who is loyal to the Beast and also who cannot be saved from that time on, 14:19-11.

But, to the contrary, if anyone now or in the Tribulation, who doesn't have the mark of the Beast, decides to receive Jesus Christ as Savior by trusting in Him (John 1:12), then nothing can separate him from the love of Christ, forever in heaven, as Romans 8:35 says. John 6:37 and 10:28-29 are corroborating verses.

No one will be able to buy or sell without the mark or name of the Beast anywhere in the world, including Israel. To receive the mark *in* Israel, itself, he or she must worship the image of the first Beast which the second Beast has the people make and put up in the temple.

The *"mark"* itself is received at the time that people worship the Beast by way of his statue or by some other indication of submission to him. This *"mark"* will probably be Satan's counterfeit of the *sealing* of the Holy Spirit for believers in this Church age (Ephesians 4:30).

The mark itself may very well be a simple, small computer chip containing all of a person's vital statistics, which will enable him to buy and sell in the upcoming cashless society, and will be inserted under the skin in the right hand or forehead. Such chips are already used on animals for purposes of identification, data and location. The first half of the Tribulation will evidently be used to prepare for all that.

The *"name of the beast"* may possibly be a form of special identification for certain classes like the clergy or priesthood of Satan.

The *"number of his name"*, we assume, is different than the *"number of the beast"*, but exactly what it is seems difficult to know. The best speculation I know of is that it may be some kind of ration book that all who get the mark of the Beast will receive.

Verse 18 tells us that the "number of the beast" is 666.

"Here is wisdom. Let him that hath understanding count the number of the beast; for it is the number of a man; and his number is six hundred three score and six. "

Man's number in the Bible is six. That he works six days and rests on the seventh is an illustration of six as his number. The tripling of the number means the deification of man, thus, the first Beast is worshipped much like the emperors of the previous Roman Empire — as god. It has been observed by some that six is short of seven, the number of perfection, and, thus, man is forever merely the creature, not the Creator, and that goes for Satan, as well.

Henry Spaak, once a member of the Common Market and Secretary General of NATO, at one time said, " *That if you send us a man who can hold the allegiance of all the people, and whether he be God or the devil, we will receive him."*

But, as Hal Lindsey, in his commentary on Revelation - *There's a New World Coming,* Vision House, 1973, Santa Ana, page 195, - says, *"Since the number 6 in the Bible stands for humanity, I believe the meaning of 666 is man trying to imitate the trinity of God (three sixes in one person). Anyone who acknowledges this blasphemous trinity by worshipping the 666 Beast will be separated forever from the true triune God."*

Any reader of this book who wants to make sure of missing out on the horrors of the Tribulation - the most terrible period in human history - may do so, right now, *before* the Rapture takes believers in Christ out of this world. It's as simple as "Believe in the Lord Jesus Christ, and you will be saved," Acts 16:31, i.e., trust in Him as God the Savior who died for you and your sins.

Chapter Three

Daniel 8:23-25 belongs just after Revelation 13 in this book on future prophetic players and events because it is an exposé on the first Beast, just as Revelation 13:1-10 was. Thus, we have *more on the first Beast*, that Roman dictator and ruler of the Revived Roman Empire, and ultimately, of the entire world.

Verse 23 is about "the king of fierce countenance", which is yet another name for the first Beast of Revelation 13.

> *"And in the latter time of their kingdom, when the transgressors are come to the full, a king of fierce countenance, and understanding dark sentences, shall stand up."*

The latter time of "their" kingdom refers to the kingdom of the four generals of Alexander the Great who took over rulership of his kingdom after his death in 323 B.C. The Roman Empire took over after their defeat of that kingdom, thus the phrase *"in the latter time of their kingdom"* identifies the time of the Roman Empire.

In the seven–year Tribulation period *"the transgressors are come to the full"*, and at that time *"a king of fierce countenance... shall stand up"* and take control of the Revived Roman Empire. No doubt one thing that makes him of *"fierce countenance"* is that he is hip deep into the occult - he *"understands dark sentences"*.

Verse 24 continues to explain why he's "of fierce countenance".

> *"And his power shall be mighty, but not by his own power; and he shall destroy wonderfully, and shall prosper, and continue, and shall destroy the mighty and the holy people."*

Another reason that he is *"of fierce countenance"* is because his mighty power comes from Satan in the last half of the Tribulation (Revelation 12:10) and from demons in the first half. The bottom line is that no matter when, it is by the power of Satan one way or the other and not by his own power.

This power will enable him to *"destroy wonderfully"*. Revelation 13:7 speaks of how he *"makes war with the saints, and to overcome them"* by making martyrs out of them. The word *"wonderful"* is far too mild, for it is anything but wonderful as we normally think of it, but it certainly will be *amazing*, for that is the meaning here.

"The mighty" that *"he shall destroy"* are *"the holy people"*. These will be Jewish people in the Tribulation. The Jews are still God's chosen people and, therefore, *"the holy people"* in the sense that God has set them apart unto Himself. They are mighty because believers in any age can *"be strong in the Lord, and in the power of his might"*, just as he commanded the believers in Ephesus to be (Ephesians 6:10).

Verse 25 gives us the deceit and demise of the king of fierce countenance.

> *"And through his policy also he shall cause deceit to prosper in his hand; and he shall magnify himself in his heart, and by peace shall destroy many; he shall also stand up against the Prince of princes, but he shall be broken without hand."*

The *"deceit"* will be to its ultimate - the abomination of desolation. The Jews in Israel will agree to place their peace and safety in the strength of the covenant that this ruler of the Revived Roman Empire said that he would *"confirm"* (strengthen), in Daniel 9:27. Now they find themselves betrayed - the treaty is shattered as far as they are concerned since they will now have to flee for their lives to the mountains of Edom, Moab and Ammon, to places like the rock hewn city of Petra in present day Jordan (Daniel 11:41 and Isaiah 26:20-21).

This deceit not only *"prospers in his hand"*, which means that it works out well for him and his program of subjection and dominance, but in the process he will *"magnify himself in his heart"* and be worshipped by all the world just as **Revelation 13:3-4** tell us: *"and all the world wondered after the beast ... and they worshipped the beast."*

Many shall be destroyed *"by peace"*, which he causes to reign in Israel in the first half of the Tribulation, but when he breaks that peace treaty (Daniel 9:27), many will be destroyed when they fail to flee and then get caught refusing to worship the image of the Beast - that statue of him placed in the Tribulation temple to be worshipped. The destruction for those in Israel will probably be by fire coming from the mouth of the statue (Revelation 13:13) or by beheading (Revelation 20:4) when distance from the statue is prohibitive. Worship of the statue of the Beast will also be associated with receiving the mark of the Beast (Revelation 13:15-16).

This *"king of fierce countenance"*, the Roman ruler of the Revived Roman Empire, fulfills the exact meaning of the Greek word "anti" when he stands up "against the Prince of princes", the Lord Jesus Christ, "King of Kings and Lord of Lords" (Revelation 19:16). Anti means *against*, and he will be against Christ to the hilt, just as Satan himself is totally against Christ in everything Christ is, stands for and spells out in His word. The Roman ruler's final stand will be at the closing battle of Armageddon when Christ comes back at His second coming to this earth where he gathers with the armies of the earth to make war against Him. Christ will destroy him and the armies and will then cast both beasts into the lake of fire (Revelation 19:19-20).

Daniel 8:25 says he will *"be broken without hands"*. That is a reference to Daniel 2:45 which depicts a stone cut out of the mountain (symbolic here of a kingdom) without hands which smashes into that final form of the Roman Empire and breaks it in pieces along with the other preceding kingdoms. This is the Bible's second and final big bang! This dramatically and violently terminates the times of the Gentiles which has been the dominating power over the Jews in the world in its system of hegemony or rulership since the time of Nebuchadnezzar.

"Without hands" means *without human intervention,* thus, God will do it on his own even though *"the armies that were in heaven follow him upon white horses, etc."* (Revelation 19:14). Verse 15 goes on to say that He does it with a sharp sword that goes out of His mouth. This is symbolic of the spoken word, which means that Jesus Christ merely speaks these enemy forces into destruction — even as He merely spoke this universe into existence (Hebrews 1:3 and Colossians 1:16 along with Genesis 1:3, 6, 9, 14, 20 and 24 where God *"said"*...).

Antiochus Ephipanes, the "little horn" of Daniel 8:9, also died without human intervention — of a foul disease. He prefigures the little horn of Daniel 7:8 who is the ruler of the Revived Roman Empire in the end times of the Tribulation.

Chapter Four

This portion of the Olivet Discourse of Jesus in Matthew 24:4-31 will help to illuminate more of the stage upon which the major players of the Tribulation perform and the future prophetic events in which the players are involved.

The discourse, in total, covers the two chapters of Matthew 24 and 25. The part that pertains to the Tribulation directly is in 24:4-31.

The setting for this discourse is the fact that Jesus has just told the scribes and Pharisees that *"your house is left unto you desolate"*, 23:38. The *"house"* was a reference to any or all of these: the temple, the nation, David's dynasty and or Jerusalem. He went so far as to tell His disciples who heard His remarks that *"There shall not be left here one stone upon another that shall not be thrown down."*

This prompted the question from them, *"Tell us, when shall these things be? And what shall be the sign of thy coming, and of the end of the age?"* The age they were referring to was the Jewish age.

The *"when"* of their question, as to the destruction of the temple, is found in Jesus' remarks in Luke 21:20-24 where He described the fall of Jerusalem in 70 A.D. with the resulting dispersion of the Jews implicit in the words of verse 24, *"and shall be led away captive into all nations; and Jerusalem shall be trodden down by the Gentiles, until the times of the Gentiles be fulfilled."*

The answer to *"what"* shall be the sign of His second coming and of the end of the Jewish age will now be answered by Him in verses 4-15. It is the abomination of desolation of verse 15, the more significant of the two great *signs* in this passage. The *second* great sign of His second coming is found in verses 27-31: *"the sign of the Son of man in heaven"*, as verse 30 says.

The first half of the Tribulation is described in verses 4-8 according to many conservative biblical scholars.

Verse 4 warns them about the deception that will be encountered.

> *"And Jesus answered and said unto them, 'Take heed that no man deceive you'."*

This is the same deception that Paul spoke of in 2 Thessalonians 2:1-2. It is deception from the Antichrist, the big lie. This was dealt with in Chapter One of this book.

Verse 5 reveals how that many false Christs shall appear.

> *"For many shall come in my name, saying, I am Christ; and shall deceive many."*

The details of this will be given in verses 23-26. This parallels the false peace of the first seal judgment of Revelation 6:1-2.

Verse 6 refers to wars and rumors of wars.

> *"And ye shall hear of wars and rumors of wars; see that ye be not troubled; for all these must come to pass, but the end is not yet."*

This parallels the warfare involved in the second seal judgment of Revelation 1:3-4. One of the wars will be the removal of three of the first horns of Daniel 7:8. These will be three nations in Europe, very likely Ireland, Greece and Denmark which currently are members of the EEC, the European Economic Community. They will evidently be too pacifistic for Beast number one, the ruler of the Revived Roman Empire, so he eliminates them from his 10 nation federation, evidently by military force or the threat of same. For further details of this scenario see Chapter Two of this book which covers the rise and fall of the first **Beast of Revelation 13:1-10**. The other wars of verse 6, here in Matthew 24, will be hot spots that seem to be part of any age. Currently, there are such hot spots in places like the Sudan and other third world countries.

Believers of the Tribulation are told not to let these things cause them to make *an outcry* ("troubled"), as W.E. Vine puts it, because they are all scheduled to happen, but the end of the Tribulation is still not yet upon them. For as verse eight says, *"All these things are the beginning of sorrows."* They are only in the first half of the Tribulation, a time of relative peace and safety, compared to the last half.

Verses 7-8 detail some of the labor pains of a new age being ushered in.

> *"For nation shall rise against nation, and kingdom against kingdom; and there shall be famines, and pesti - lences, and earthquakes, in various places. (8) All these are the beginning of sorrows."*

This describes the relative peace of the first half of the Tribulation, in relation to the last half, as nations vie for power. It also describes the power struggle depicted in Revelation 6:2, the first seal, and also as in Daniel 7:8.

The *"famines"* are described in more detail in the third seal of Revelation 6:5-6. *"Pestilences"*, deadly infections, like the current ebolla outbreaks in Africa, can accompany famines which weaken the immune system in people and make them more susceptible. The super resistant strains to antibiotics, currently on the increase, are one class of those deadly infections.

Coming events cast their shadows, and we are living in the shadows on this side of the Tribulation, regarding earthquakes. They have increased in number and intensity in recent years and will continue to do so even into the first half of the Tribulation. They will reach their maximum intensity at the end of the Tribulation as part of the seventh bowl of wrath judgment of Revelation 16:17-21. At that time there will be *a great earthquake such as was not since men were upon the earth"*, 16:18. It will not only divide the *"great city"* (Jerusalem of 11:8) into three parts and fell the cities of the nations, but as verse 19 indicates, will radically change the topography of the earth: *"And every island fled away, and the mountains were not found."* This well may be part of the Lord's refurbishing of the earth for the Millennial Kingdom, for it happens just prior to it.

But, there is also the possibility that an earthquake was the closest thing the ancient prophet and apostle could come up with to describe or symbolize the global destruction that an allout nuclear war would bring. Hal Lindsey goes into the details of such a conflagration in *The Final Battle*, his most recent (1995) book.

The second half of the Tribulation, known as the Great Tribulation, is in view in verses 9-14 of Matthew 24 according to the view of many conservative biblical scholars.

Verses 9-10 speak of the persecution of believers by Beast number one.

> *"Then shall they deliver you up to be afflicted, and shall kill you; and ye shall be hated of all nations for my name's sake. (10) And then shall many be offended, and shall betray one another."*

The *persecution* and *hatred* of believers are covered in more detail in Revelation 12 and 13:5-7 and mentioned in 6:9-11. There, the persecution and hatred take the specific forms of martyrdom (6:9-11) and death (12:11), persecution (12:13) and war with the saints (12:17; 13:7). Matthew 25:37-44 speaks of *hunger, thirst, privation, prison* and *sickness* as other forms of persecution.

Verse 10 indicates that many will be *ensnared* ("offended") by the ones who shall *"betray"* them. The unsaved Jews in Israel, and in the world for that matter, will *"hate"* their fellow Jews who are believers and will betray them by turning them in, history's greatest manhunt.

Verse 11 tells of false prophets arising to deceive many.

> *"And many false prophets shall arise, and shall deceive many."*

The *"false prophets"* will no doubt be apostate Jews who will be promulgators and teachers of worldwide ecumenical religion sponsored and promoted by the ruler of the Revived Roman Empire, Beast number one. A spiritually blind person, as these will be, shall easily be deceived as to who really is God, what His program is and what really happened to the multiplied millions that suddenly vanished from the earth at the Rapture.

Verse 12 speaks of the love of many growing cold.

> *"And because iniquity shall abound, the love of many shall grow cold."*

The *"iniquity"* that abounds is *lawlessness*, for that is the precise meaning of the Greek word translated "iniquity" here. God's divine laws of establishment like marriage, freedom and law and order will have broken down, and believers will not be able to stand the pressure of such breakdown. This will cause their love for others (*"love for many"*) to *"grow cold"*; their zeal for evangelism cools.

Verse 13 refers to the deliverance of those who endure to the end.

> *"But he that shall endure unto the end; the same shall be saved."*

Those who *"endure to the end"* are the ones who don't cop out when the going gets tough and who wait for *"the end"* of the Tribulation with a sense of expectancy, but above all, who stay alive. Such ones will be *"saved"*, which means physically delivered by the Lord's return at the end of the Tribulation.

Verse 14 reveals that the gospel will be preached in all the world before the end of the Tribulation comes.

> *"And this gospel of the kingdom shall be preached in all the world for a witness unto all nations; and then shall the end come."*

The gospel of the kingdom" includes the same message about the death, burial and resurrection of Christ that Paul gave us in 1 Corinthians 15:1-4, but in the Tribulation there is the urgency of the shortness of time, and that the Millennial Kingdom is next on God's agenda.

Through the ones preaching it, God will make sure that the gospel reaches all the nations in the world. God's witnesses will be the untouchable 144,000 Jews, 12,000 from each tribe, the two witnesses of Revelation 14:12-13 and an *"angel flying in the midst of heaven, having the everlasting gospel to preach unto them that dwell on the earth, and to every nation, and kindred, and tongue, and people."* (**Revelation 14:6**). All these witnesses will make the Tribulation period the greatest time of evangelism and witness of all time as alluded to in Revelation 7:9.

Verses 15-26 contain a repetition and an enlargement of the last half of the Tribulation.

Verse 15 is a warning about the abomination of desolation.

> *"When ye, therefore, shall see the abomination of deso -*
> *lation, spoken by Daniel the prophet, stand in the holy*
> *place (whosoever readeth, let him understand)."*

They don't visually have to *"see"* the abomination of desolation, that image or statue of the first Beast of Revelation 13. All they have to do is to *understand* that it is in the holy place to be worshipped. Someone else could have seen it, and as word gets around, others who haven't actually seen it will *understand* that it is there.

Daniel 9:27 speaks of it as *"The overspreading of abominations...poured upon the desolate".* That same verse says that *"in the midst of the week he shall cause the sacrifice and the oblation to cease."* The reason it will cease is because it will replace with an idol the Levitical system of worship the Jews had used in previous centuries. Satan's plan for them is to worship an idol instead of Jesus Christ.

The covenant that Daniel 9:27 says is *"confirmed"* will be the treaty of peace and safety in the land of Israel that Beast number one, the ruler of the Revived Roman Empire, actually *strengthens*, for that is the meaning of the Hebrew word translated *"confirmed"* here. Evidently, he will simply put teeth — military and political clout — in the peace treaty that will be already in place by the time of the Tribulation or immediately thereafter. Such a treaty is now in place with the exception of Syria, which is currently negotiating. It is expected to complete the loop soon — within a year or two, but to be realistic, as past history teaches, it could be delayed by something, like terrorist attacks on Israelis.

As recently as December 26th, 1996, *The Associated Press* released the following news story. **Netanyahu: 'No doubt' on peace with**

Syria. *Jerusalem* — Prime Minister Benjamin Netanyahu promised Wednesday that he will be the Israeli leader to forge peace with Syria. *"I have no doubt that we will succeed in the mission of achieving peace with Syria in this government's present term,"* Netanyahu told legislators in Israel's parliament. But Netanyahu also suggested he was not backing away from his opposition to Syria's demand that Israel return the entire *Golan Heights*, which it captured in 1967. *" Peace that does not provide the basic requirments (of) ensuring our security and water supply is a recipe for the continuation of the conflict,"* he said.

Verse 16 is a warning to flee when the statue is in place.

> *"Then let them who are in Judea flee into the mountains."*

With this statue in the holy place to be worshipped, the Jews who are offended by the insistence that they worship an idol, will know that their peace treaty has just fallen apart for them, and they will be quite open to an escape plan. They get it in the form of this warning to flee to the mountains.

God is going to protect them supernaturally for three and one-half years in those mountains of Edom, Moab and Ammon, where Jordan is today, just as it implies in Daniel 11:41 when Israel is invaded by the king of the north. Matthew 24:21-26 will give us an idea of some of the pressures the Jews will be under even while they wait it out in the mountains under the protection and provision of God, Revelation 12:6.

Verses 17-20 underscore the desperate urgency of their flight out of Jerusalem and to the mountains.

> *"Let him who is on the housetop not come down to take anything out of his house; (18) Neither let him who is in the field return back to take his clothes. (19) And woe unto those who are with child, and to those who nurse children in those days! (20) But pray that your flight be not in the winter, neither on the sabbath day;"*

From the moment the abomination of desolation is put in place, all who refuse to worship it will be slain, just as Revelation 13:14-15 indicates. It will be immediately and ruthlessly enforced.

Those who choose to flee will not even be able to take the time to come downstairs and pack. If the one who flees finds himself in his field, he won't be able to take time to return to his house so

he can pack his clothes. He will need all the lead time he can get
if he hopes to avoid being caught and killed by those in authority
under both Beasts, one and two.

If the flight should take place in the winter, the problem of bad
weather would greatly hinder them, and if on the sabbath day, the
traffic would slow them down. But it is interesting to note that the
Church does not worship on the sabbath. This might well be a
subtle hint that the Church is not on earth at this time because it
was raptured at the start of the Tribulation.

**Verse 21 gives us the name of and source for the last half of
the Tribulation — the Great Tribulation.**

> *"For then shall be great tribulation, such as was
> not since the beginning of the world to this time,
> no, nor ever shall be."*

Here is the verse from which and by which the Great
Tribulation gets its name. The abomination of desolation begins
the greatest and most intense period of suffering in the entire
history of God's people. All the events and judgments of the
seals, trumpets and bowls are included in this verse.

**Verse 22 states that the days of the Great Tribulation will be
shortened.**

> *"And except those days should be shortened, there
> should no flesh be saved; but for the elect's sake
> those days shall be shortened."*

Because of the severity and intensity of the suffering in the
Great Tribulation, God will shorten those days in number, not in
length. They will still be 24 hour days. The only way any will be
able to survive physically, i.e., literally be *"saved"* or delivered
from physical death will be because of this limit on the *number* of
days in the Great Tribulation.

But God makes it clear that He *"shortens"* those days for the
sake of preserving His elect so that He will have a living remnant
of some to go immediately into and populate the Millennial
Kingdom, alive, at the end of the Tribulation.

**Verses 23-26 indicate the kind of pressure and temptation
those who have fled to the mountains will receive.**

> *"Then if any man shall say unto you, Lo,
> here is Christ, or there; believe it not.
> (24) For there shall arise false Christs,*

and false prophets, and shall show great signs and wonders, insomuch that, if it were possible, they shall deceive the very elect. (25) Behold I have told you before. (26) Wherefore, if they shall say unto you, Behold, he is in the desert; go not forth: behold, he is in the secret chambers; believe it not."

There have been many who have claimed to be Christ the Messiah all the way from Charles Manson to the Reverend Moon, and there will evidently arise in the Tribulation false Christs in addition to the false prophet who claims to be the Messiah of Israel.

The fugitive Jews in the mountains will be tempted by such ones, but they are warned to *"believe it not"*, and the implication is that if they will hunker down and stay in the mountains, they will survive. To give in to the deception will be to expose themselves and be captured because they left the supernatural protection and provision God had graciously provided for them.

The temptation will be a test to see if they believe God's promise to them in **Isaiah 26:20-21**:

"Come, my people, enter thou into they chambers, and shut thy doors about thee; hide thyself as it were for a little moment, until the indignation is past. (21) For, behold, the Lord cometh out of his place to punish the inhabitants of the earth for their iniquity; the earth also shall disclose her blood, and shall no more cover her slain."

The *"chambers"* of verse 20 and the shutting of the doors and hiding for a little moment refer to staying in the mountains where they'll be safe for the last half of the Tribulation.

It looks like it is possible that some who have fled will be able to be deceived because the *"if"* in verse 24 is a first class conditional if which means that, yes, it is possible.

Just because they will be supernaturally protected and provided for does not necessarily mean that demons will be kept from infiltrating this mountainous stronghold. The mention of *"great signs and wonders"* among them strongly suggests that there will be Jews among this group of refugees who will expose themselves to demonic deception by perhaps getting restless and wanting something more and greater than God's Word. When anyone wants more than what God has provided, Satan and his demons are always waiting in the wings to come to center stage and see that they get it — even if it's in the form of the supernatural.

The second great sign of Christ's coming at His second advent is found in verses 27-30.

Verse 27 emphasizes the suddenness of His second coming.

> *"For as the lightning cometh out of the east, and shineth even unto the west, so shall also the coming of the Son of man be."*

One thing universally true about lightning is its *suddenness*. It gives no warning or advance notice — it's just instantaneously there in a flash. Christ's second coming to this earth will be that sudden and will be seen from east to west.

Verse 36 says, *"But of that day and hour knoweth no man, no not the angels of heaven, but my Father only."* Believers during the Tribulation will be able to keep track of the time, either from the date of the Rapture (seven years), or the date of the abomination of desolation (three and one–half years), and be able to know of the time of His second coming to all but the day and hour, i.e., the hours of the day. In that sense it will be *sudden.*

Verse 28 pictures judgment accompanying His second advent.

> *For wherever the carcass is, there will the eagles be gathered together."*

The *"carcass"* indicates the *bodies* of the soldiers of the armies converged at Armageddon. These will be slain in the millions by the sword of His mouth as Revelation 19:15 and 19 tell us, and that His garments are red from treading in the winefat of the winepress alone and trampling them all in the fury of His anger for vengeance is in His heart, as Isaiah 63:1-6 says. The apostle John adds the fact that *"blood came out of the winepress, even unto the horses bridles, by the space of a thousand and six hundred furlongs"* **Revelation 14:20**. The blood of men will run so deep in that 200–mile battleground called a winepress by John, and Isaiah that it will spatter to the height of the bridle of a horse. What carnage! If it turns out to be literally "to the bridles," it'll be even worse.

The *"eagles"* of Matthew 24:28 are buzzards or vultures, which are symbolic of death and destruction, here and elsewhere.

Verse 29 gives us the backdrop for the second coming.

> *"Immediately after the tribulation of those days*
> *shall the sun be darkened, and the moon shall not*
> *give its light, and the stars shall fall from heaven,*
> *and the powers of the heavens shall be shaken."*

No matter how the darkness occurs - supernaturally or by a nuclear winter - just before Christ comes back to plant His feet on the Mount of Olives and be welcomed by the 144,000 in Revelation 14:1, He is preceded by the kind of darkness that is there before the curtain goes up to begin a Broadway production of some kind. Only, in this case, if it is supernaturally produced, He himself will throw the switch to darken the sun, moon and stars, and even to the shaking of the powers of the heavens (possibly a reference to demons being removed from this earth). Isaiah 13:10 and Joel 2:30-31 mention such a celestial darkness.

But how appropriate this dark backdrop is in order to properly dramatize the One who is the Light of the World. It will focus the attention where it belongs, then and always, on Him who is *"the true Light, which lighteth every man that cometh into the world"* (**John 1:9**).

Verse 30 gives the appearance of the second great sign.

> *"And then shall appear the sign of the Son of man*
> *in the heaven; and then shall all the tribes of the*
> *earth mourn, and they shall see the Son of man*
> *coming in the clouds of heaven with power and*
> *great glory."*

A *"sign"*, basically, is a visible miracle that is designed by God to convey a message of some kind. The message in this case is that the King of Kings and Lord of Lords (Revelation 19:16) is standing in the wings ready to take center stage in His glorious, prophetic second coming.

The sign itself is the subject of some fascinating speculation. Let me share four of the most likely ones with you:

1. It is *"clouds"* of saints that accompany His second return, as verse 30 states.
2. It is the same *star sign*, Virgo, at His birth (Numbers 24:17) in the constellation Coma. The wise men followed that star to Jerusalem, then to Bethlehem.
3. It is the Shekinah Glory which may be used to identify

Him as the God of Israel.
4. It is the New Jerusalem descending like a satellite from the third heaven to hover over the millennial earth for 1,000 years (Revelation 14:3 21:1-2,10). (From class notes at Dallas Theological Seminery under J. Dwight Pentecost, 1968)

When *"all the tribes of the earth shall mourn"* upon seeing Christ coming back, it'll be as **Zechariah 12:10-14** says. Verse 10 explicitly says *"they shall look upon me whom they have pierced, and they shall mourn for him, as one mourneth for his only son, and shall be in bitterness for his firstborn."*

"They shall see the Son of man coming in the clouds of heaven with power and great glory". The clouds of heaven seem to be the resurrected saints of all ages to this point (Daniel 12:23,13). The following verses refer to Him coming in the clouds: Matthew 26:64; Jude 14; Revelation 1:7; Daniel 7:13 and Hebrews 12:1 speak of a cloud of witnesses. When you combine all that with the verses that say He's coming back with all the saints, as in Zechariah 14:5 and Colossians 3:4, you are left with the compelling conclusion that the clouds of heaven are the resurrected saints of all ages to that moment. This will make front row seats at the theater seem like last row bleachers at the Super Bowl, even though we, too, will be spectators. The *"power"* and *"glory"* will belong exclusively to the *"Son of Man"*. We will not be able, or permitted, to lift a finger to help Him do what is His sole right and duty to do.

Verse 31 is Israel's last roundup.

"And he shall send his angels with a great sound of a trumpet, and they shall gather together his elect from the four winds, from one end of heaven to the other."

God's angels will have the job of rounding up *"God's elect"* of Israel from the four corners of the earth, *"four winds"* or *"the uttermost part of the earth to the uttermost part of heaven"*, meaning the winds of the first heaven, earth's atmosphere, as Mark 13:27 indicates. They will evidently be transported from the four corners of the earth supernaturally, perhaps much like Phillip when he went from Samaria to Gaza (Acts 8:26, 27, 39).

God wants His chosen people to be in the chosen land of Palestine when it comes time for Him to fulfill all of His covenants to Israel, which He will do at the beginning of the millennium.

Chapter Five

Daniel 11:36-45 is a passage of scripture that gives us a bird's–eye view of the invasion of Israel by first Kings of the the South, then the North, East and West in what will turn out to be the campaign of Armageddon, the final battle to be fought in the last half of the Tribulation, just prior to the second coming of Jesus Christ to this earth.

Verses 36 -37 give us a description of the Antichrist and the policy he follows as dictator of Israel.

> *"And the king shall do according to his will; and he shall exalt himself, and magnify himself above every god, and shall speak marvelous things against the God of gods, and shall prosper till the indignation be accomplished; for that which is determined shall be done. (37) Neither shall he regard the gods of his fathers, nor the desire of women, nor regard any god: for he shall magnify himself above all."*

This *"king"* is an illustration of Antiochus Epiphanes who per-
secuted the Jews in the days of the Maccabean revolt in the second
century B.C. The Antichrist will also similarly persecute the Jews
in the latter days, during the Tribulation.

This *"king"* is the one we identified in Chapter One of this
book as *the Antichrist, the willful king, the false prophet, an
hireling shepherd, the worthless shepherd* and *the second beast of
Revelation 13.* He will be the *dictator of Israel* just like the first
beast of Revelation 13 will be the *dictator* of the Revived Roman
Empire in the first half of the Tribulation and in the last half - the
entire world.

"He shall do according to his will" is the basis for one of his
names being *the willful king.* He wants to do what he thinks is
best, regardless of what God has said in His Word about anything.
He is totally self-centered and does or promotes only what
enhances *his* interests. He is *"against the God of gods".* John
said *"that antichrist shall come* (and) *even now there are many
antichrists,"* (1 **John 2:18**) and *"He is antichrist, that denieth the
Father and the Son"* (1 **John 2:22**). This end-time Antichrist
even speaks "marvelous things against God", verse 36, which the
NIV says are "unheard-of" or "astonishing" as in the Amplified
Version. It is no stretch to say that he will have a blasphemous
mouth.

He will *"prosper"* or succeed in his abominable plans and
ways until *"the indignation be accomplished; for that which is
determined shall be done."* This means he'll succeed until the end
of the Tribulation which will come to its *scheduled* end, for God is
in control and is allowing the two beasts one last fling, all of
which accomplishes His plan and purposes.

Some evidence that the second Beast will be a Jew is found in
verse 37. He does not regard the *"gods of his fathers, nor the
desire of women."* *"Gods"* is plural here because the Jews have
worshipped false gods (Joshua 24:15) as well as the one true God.
"The desire of women" that he will have no regard for is
commonly thought by many sound interpreters to be the desire of
Jewish women, especially those of the tribe of Judah, to be the
mother of the Messiah. In Haggai 2:7 the Messiah is also spoken
of as "the desire", this time *"the desire of all nations".*

It is difficult to believe that the one who claims to be the
Messiah in the Tribulation could be anything *other* than a Jew.
The strong possibility that he will be of the tribe of Dan is further
reason to believe he will be a Jew. A proper understanding of

Revelation 7:4-8, Amos 8:14, and Genesis 49:16,17 and how they all relate to each other on this issue would add further evidence. It evidently won't matter to the Tribulation Jews that this "Messiah" (the Antichrist) is not from the tribe of Judah.

He will not only *"exalt himself above every god"* by *"sitting in the temple of God showing himself that he is God,"* as 2 Thessalonians 2:4 says, but he will *"not regard any god; for he shall magnify himself above all"*, verse 37 of Daniel 11 says. It would appear from this statement that the Antichrist, at first, will recognize no other god but himself — thinking that he himself is god — but will change his mind a little later on in order to placate and cooperate with the first Beast, the reason for which we will see in verse 38.

Verse 38 speaks of the policy of the Antichrist with other nations abroad.

> *"But in his estate shall he honor the god of fortresses; and a god whom his fathers knew not shall he honor with gold, and silver, and with precious stones, and pleasant things."*

No matter which way he turns to look for a foreign friend that he thinks is trustworthy enough for him, surrounded as he is in a hostile crowd, he finds the closest possibility in the west under its dictator of the Revived Roman Empire. After entering into the Daniel 9:27 covenant under the Roman dictator guaranteeing Israel peace and safety in its land, the Antichrist, a little later on, decides to enhance the peace treaty by honoring *"the god of fortresses"* in agreeing to put a statue of him in the temple to be worshipped (Matthew 24:15).

Then, to support the trade agreement that the Roman dictator makes with him in order to strengthen his economic hand, the Antichrist will be willing to honor *"a god whom his fathers knew not ... with gold, and silver, and with precious stones, and pleasant things."* He'll do this *"in his estate"*, or in his *authority* as a dictator, but the price he'll pay will be in *"gold, and silver"* (money) and more than likely valuable metals rather than *"precious stones"*. *"Pleasant things"* may very well be natural resources such as what we know are there today — oil very deep under Israel's soil and super abundant chemicals from its Dead Sea. These resources will attract the attention of those who aren't included in the deal — the North, East and South — and just may be the thing that triggers the South's invasion of Israel, followed by the North, East and the West in order to protect their interests so that they don't get left holding the short end of the stick.

"The god of fortresses" is the Roman dictator and leader of the Revived Roman Empire who leads this military, political and economic powerhouse in the world of that day. As to being a god, the Roman dictator will be deified by the Antichrist in keeping with emperor worship of the old Roman Empire. This, of course, is *"a god whom his fathers knew not"*. The God of the fathers of the Antichrist was the living and true God of Israel — Jesus Christ, Jehovah, yet the Antichrist will not honor Him, but will honor the Roman dictator as god.

Verse 39 speaks of how the Antichrist rules the land of Israel.

> *"Thus shall he do in the strongest fortresses with a foreign god whom he shall acknowledge and increase with glory; and he shall cause them to rule over many, and shall divide the land for gain."*

"The strongest fortresses" refer to Israel being divided into the strongest possible military zones. The Antichrist, dictator of Israel, realizes that he can't meet all the military needs he has for the security of his land, so he relies on the peace treaty of Daniel 9:27 combined with the military might of the dictator of the Revived Roman Empire to put teeth into this treaty.

Israel has for many years spent about 50 percent of its income on defense and will welcome the relief this treaty will give so that Israel can do what Ezekiel said it would do — dwell safely and at rest in the land of unwalled villages having neither bars nor gates, Ezekiel 38:11. This the Israeli dictator will do *"with a foreign god,"* the deified first Beast of Revelation 13, *"whom he shall acknowledge and increase with glory,"* verse 39.

Part of the Antichrist's rule in Israel will be to divide the land into economic zones for the most gain economically, as well as militarily, something which the genius of the Antichrist will have little trouble concocting. It looks like he will get his pals, *"them to rule over many"* into power in these military and economic zones. In the Old Testament, Israel was divided geographically by tribal boundaries. Since he's presented himself as their Messiah, maybe he'll use the tribal borders as boundaries of the zones.

Verse 40 chronicles the beginning of the campaign of Armageddon.

> *"And at the time of the end shall the king of the south push at him; and the king of the north shall come against him like a whirlwind, with chariots, and with horsemen, and with many ships; and he shall enter into the countries, and shall overflow and pass through."*

"*At the time of the end*" refers to the last half of the Tribulation, specifically the worst part of it. *The king of the south* refers to Egypt which will invade Israel in order to "*take a spoil*", in the words of Ezekiel 38:13. The mineral resources of the Dead Sea have been estimated in the trillions of dollars. In addition to that, oil has been discovered very deep under the soil of Israel rivaling the oil reserves under Saudia Arabia. At the present time it is not economically feasible to bring it to the surface, but by that time it well may be. Even if it isn't, Israel is considered by the Arabs, as well as poverty stricken Russia, as it exists today, to be a wealthy land. Added to all that is the prospect of a year–round, warm water sea port in Israel. She presently does not have one.

Egypt will push at "*him*" — the false prophet, Beast number two, the Antichrist — in a military invasion. Right now Egypt has one of the world's biggest armies — sizable enough, at any rate, to give this a try. Egypt will be goaded into this by demonic forces (Revelation 16:14, 16) in addition to its own greed.

"*The King of the North*", Russia and its allies of Ezekiel 38:1-6, will not want to be beat out of such a rich prize so it launches a counter invasion from the north with great speed "*like a whirlwind, with chariots, and with horsemen.*" "*Chariots*" was the ancient prophet's term for what he saw as a tank, and "*horsemen*" refers to other armored vehicles including personnel carriers and jeeps with the mobility they all have in modern warfare.

"*With many ships*" indicates that the Russian fleet will come into the Mediterranean from the Black Sea through the Bosphorus to engage what would be, if it were to occur today, the U.S. Sixth Fleet. Russia's land army could come through Turkey or Syria, two of its likely allies. The west, under the dictator of the Revived Roman Empire, will evidently be unaware of either invasion due to a blackout of communications caused by God's fifth bowl of wrath, judgment poured out "*upon the throne of the beast*" causing his kingdom to be *"full of darkness"*, as Revelation 16:10 says.

This darkness in Rome will allow that *"he"*, the King of the North (Russia), be able to *"enter into the countries"* of the middle east, like Turkey or Syria and Lebanon, and rapidly control the main routes for travel in those countries in order to set things up to *"pass through"* Israel and keep advancing on and into Egypt.

Verse 41 reveals three countries of that area which escape overthrow.

> *"He shall enter also into the glorious land, and many countries shall be overthrown, but these shall escape out of his hand, even Edom, and Moab, and the chief of the children of Ammon."*

"He," the King of the North, shall enter into *"the glorious land,"* the land of Israel, and in the process will *"overthrow many."* The word *"countries"* is not in the Hebrew text so it may just refer to many people.

But the countries that *"escape"* being overthrown in this invasion of Palestine are *"Edom, Moab and Ammon,"* where the nation of Jordan is today. This is the same mountainous country the Jews were warned to flee to in Matthew 24:15-16 when the statue of the first beast of Revelation 13 is placed in the Tribulation temple to be worshipped. Isaiah 26:20-21 refers to this same hiding place where the Lord will supernaturally protect all who flee Jerusalem for three and one-half years because of the image of the Beast in the temple. So we see that it is God who keeps the King of the North from overthrowing Edom, Moab and Ammon, keeping them as a hiding place for His people. This is just another indication that our God is always in control.

Devout Jews got the idolatry cure good and solid during Israel's 70-year captivity in Babylon starting about 586 B.C. So those who believe God's Word will not hesitate to flee when they see that statue, or idol, in the temple. Matthew 24:21-26 goes into some of the things the Jews will experience while in hiding during the last half of the Tribulation. This scene was detailed in Chapter Three of this book.

Verse 42 indicates that Egypt shall not escape.

> *"He shall stretch forth his hand also upon the*
> *countries, and the land of Egypt shall not escape."*

The King of the North, Russia and its allies, as we have already read, invades *"the countries"* of the area by way of such countries as possibly Turkey, Syria and Lebanon, but it looks like Egypt is one of the primary objectives. The north must shut down the south, which triggered these invasions of the land of Israel in the first place.

Verse 43 tells us of the King of the North's success in Africa.

> *"But he shall have power over the treasures of gold*
> *and silver, and over all the precious things of Egypt;*
> *and the Libyans and the Ethiopians shall be at his*
> *steps."*

"He", once again, is the King of the North, and we find that he will be able, by his *"power"*, to control whatever wealth Egypt may have in that day. The invasion will have been completed by the land and naval forces of the North and some exploitation of the spoils of victory is taking place, *"gold, silver and precious things of Egypt."*

But we also see here, a further dimension to Russia's greed: Libya and Ethiopia are in the crosshairs of Russia's sights pertaining to Africa. That's the meaning of *"at his steps."* Russia could also well use the natural resources of the rest of Africa and the wealth it could bring. In fact, its *strategy* in recent years has been the exploitation of certain portions of Africa, including Egypt under Nasser, but such efforts failed each time.

Verse 44 reveals that someone from the east wants in on the spoils.

> *"But tidings out of the east and out of the north shall*
> *trouble him; therefore, he shall go forth with great*
> *fury to destroy, and utterly to sweep away many."*

"Tidings out of the east" that trouble the King of the North would no doubt be the invasion launched by Orientals, like China, which has the largest standing army in the world today. In that day, the size of it will be in the multiplied millions. It is the invasion from the east by a super large human army that takes

advantage of the Euphrates river being dried up so the army can walk across it, Revelation 16:12. I understand there is a dam at the headwaters of the Euphrates in Turkey and that there is also now a road from China through the Himalayas of Kashmir to Pakistan. The rest of the passage, verses 13-16, describes how demons will work on the kings of the earth to draw them (hooks in their jaws, as Ezekiel 38:4 put it) to the battle of Armageddon.

This invasion from the east would seem to be that which is referred to in Isaiah 63:1-6 and 34:6 from Edom and from Bozrah in present day Jordan where the eastern army would have to cross to get into Israel. The slaughter described there is the final battle of Armageddon, especially where the eastern army will be destroyed by the Lord.

The King of the North will turn back from Egypt to head off the threat of the east to cut him off and isolate him from his own country and supplies. He will also do this to counter the *"tidings out of the north"* (This time "north" is not referring to Russia).

North of Egypt is the Mediterranean Sea which hosts the fleet of the west, currently the U.S. Sixth Fleet, and at that time the Russian fleet which is part of the North's invasion force. But now it looks like the West's fleet under the first Beast, the dictator of the Revived Roman Empire, sails in north of Egypt to block Russia from further help by her naval forces supplying her. No doubt a naval battle ensues with the west winning it. Right now Russia's fleet is no match for the U.S. Sixth Fleet.

The West, evidently, is literally in the dark about the invasions of Israel by the North and the South due to the fifth bowl of wrath having been *"poured out upon the throne of the beast"* and shrouding his kingdom *"full of darkness"*, to use the language of Revelation 16:10. When the darkness lifts and the West's communications are restored, the West responds to the invasions as indicated above.

The response of the King of the North to this threat from the east and the naval battle to the north of Egypt will be with *"great fury to destroy, and utterly to sweep away many."* He throws everything he's got into an effort to get back to Israel before he can be cut off. It's a case of destroy or be destroyed.

Verse 45 indicates that the King of the North succeeds, yet fails.

"And he shall plant the tabernacles of his palace between the seas in the glorious holy mountain; yet he shall come to his end, and none shall help him."

The *"tabernacles of his palace"* is a reference to "his royal tents" as the NIV translates this, and no doubt refers to his military command center. He places it *"between the seas"* — Dead Sea and Mediterranean Sea — which is where Jerusalem is located. *"In the glorious holy mountain"* further identifies the location as Jerusalem because Mt. Zion is that holy mountain, and Mt. Zion is also a synonym for Jerusalem.

The King of the North's *failure* comes from the fact that his end, or destruction, takes place in the final battle of Armageddon where *"none shall help him"* because *"out of His mouth* (the Lord Jesus Christ) *goeth a sharp sword, that with it He should smite the nations, and He shall rule them with a rod of iron; and He treadeth the winepress of the fierceness and wrath of Almighty God. And He hath on His vesture and on His thigh a name written, KING OF KINGS, AND LORD OF LORDS,"* **Revelation 19:15-16**. Any help from human armies is also destroyed at this time.

Further details as to the carnage involved may be found in that same chapter, Revelation 19:17-19. Joel 3:9-17 also describes the scene, but no passage is as extensive as Ezekiel 38 and 39 which cover the North's part in all this, exclusively. Chapter Six of this book will detail those two chapters verse by verse.

Chapter Six

God Spotlights Russia's Part in the Invasion of Israel

This chapter begins the exposé of *the third major player* in the Tribulation. The first two players were exposed in the previous chapters. Ezekiel 38 and 39 give us a rather detailed but isolated account of the destruction, or judgment, of a country to the north of Israel that we know by the name of Russia, but which is called in the Bible, *"the land of Magog"* (Ezekiel 38:2). The focus in these two chapters is on the destruction of Russia and its allies.

From the language of Revelation 19:17-19 we conclude that this judgment occurs in the campaign of Armageddon at the very end of the Great Tribulation. This is God's viewpoint of Russia's part in that great battle. The passage speaks of the carnage of the battle in symbols of fowl eating the flesh of kings, captains, mighty men and horses.

The same kind of language is used by Ezekiel, yet in neither passage is it literally flesh being eaten because 39:20 says that those fowl shall be filled with horses and *chariots*. As tough as a buzzard's gizzard is, he still can't choke down a chariot, so we must assume that this is a divine clue for us to take such words symbolically.

But this does not mean that we are not, therefore, following a literal interpretation of the Bible. To interpret it symbolically when there is such good evidence to warrant it, fulfills the true *meaning of a literal interpretation.* To interpret it literally, in spite of such clues, would be to follow what Bible students derisively call *wooden literalism.* Therefore, this language of the fowl eating the flesh is *symbolic of the total destruction* that will take place at the battle of Armageddon at the end of the Tribulation.

Some of the other passages in Scripture that describe this same battle, or campaign, but do not exclusively, or necessarily, focus on *the destruction of Russia,* are Daniel 11:36-45; Revelation 14:14-20; 16:12-16; 19:17-19; Zechariah 12 and 14; Isaiah 63:1-6 and Joel 3:9-21.

Daniel 11 describes the invasion of Israel by the North in the last half of the Tribulation, but includes the military activities of Egypt of the *south* as well as those of the *eastern* and *western* powers.

Verses 1-3 of Ezekiel 38 identify Russia as the invader.

"And the word of the Lord came unto me saying, (2) Son of man, set thy face against Gog, of the land of Magog, the chief prince of Meshech and Tubal, and prophesy against him, (3) And say, Thus saith the Lord God: Behold, I am against thee, O Gog, the chief prince of Meshech and Tubal."

The term *"son of man"* is a reference to Ezekiel that is used some 90 times in this book.

"Gog" refers to the leader of the land of Russia called *"Magog",* here. Gog is the *"prince"* or leader of Rosh ("chief"), which is the name for the ancient Scythians who lived north of the Caspian Sea and northeast of the Black Sea. Gog is also prince of the land of *"Meshech and Tubal",* otherwise known as southern Ukraine.

This prophecy is against *"him", "Gog",* the *leader* of Russia. One of its leaders by the name of Joseph Stalin once boasted, "We have deposed the czars of the earth, we shall now dethrone the Lord of Heaven." Also from Moscow has come this statement: "Our rocket has by-passed the moon. It is nearing the sun, and we have not discovered God. We have turned out lights in heaven that no man will be able to put on again. We are breaking the yoke of the Gospel, the opium of the masses. Let us go forth, and Christ shall be relegated to mythology."

Is it any wonder that Russia is the special object of God's judgment in the form of the destruction that these chapters describe?

Verses 4-6 identify Russia's allies in the invasion.

> *"And I will turn thee back and put hooks into thy jaws, and I will bring thee forth, and all thine army, horses, and horsemen, all of them clothed with all sorts of armor, even a great company with bucklers and shields, all of them handling swords: (5) Persia, Cush, and Put with them with shields and helmet; (6) Gomer, and all its hordes; the house of Togarmah of the north quarters, and all its hordes; and many peoples with thee."*

God describes, here, how He will get them all to invade Israel by saying *"I will turn thee back."* Literally this phrase says "I will lead you away" from Russia and her allies; away from their homelands and into Israel by putting *"hooks into thy jaws and I will bring thee forth."* That will happen no matter who Russia's leader is.

Here is a list of the baited hooks that God is even now preparing:

1. Russia has long sought a warm-water seaport that would give her access to the waterways of the world. The port of Haifa would give her that.
2. The oil deposits under Israel are very deep under her soil, and are about as vast as those of Saudia Arabia but just the thing needed to rescue the basket case economy that exists in Russia today. Perhaps the technology to extract that oil economically will be on the line by the time of this invasion. I heard on the news (May, 96) that they are looking into extraction technology that can take them twice as deep as today.
3. The chemical deposits of the Dead Sea are so great they have been estimated in the trillions of dollars.

The army of horses and horsemen with bucklers and shields and swords, I believe, is Ezekiel's symbolic way of describing the modern army. It was his way of describing it because he had no knowledge of modern weapons.

The allies of Russia are listed in verses 5 and 6.

"Persia" is present day Iran, Iraq, Syria, Afghanistan, Pakistan and Yemen. All of these countries *may* be included as allies of Russia. *"Cush"* and *"Put"* refer to *Ethiopia* and *Libya* in Africa. *"Gomer"* refers to the area of the *Ukraine* or *eastern Germany*.

"Togarmah" seems to be a reference to the Armenians who once lived north of Israel in present day *Turkey*. *"North quarters"* is the Hebrew word for *"far north"* or the northern recesses of Russia. This would take in all the rest of Russia not included in these other areas of Russia such as Rosh, Meshech and Tubal.

Students of prophecy should be indebted to Hal Lindsey, in his latest book *The Final Battle* (Hal Lindsey, *The Final Battle*, Western Front, Ltd., Palos Verdes, 1995, page 184), for bringing us all up to speed as to the identity of the Arab allies that will accompany Russia in the invasion and the incredible total numbers of the combined forces — 10 million! The number of planes and tanks they now have is also chilling — 24,000 tanks and 3,880 combat aircraft — giving new and current meaning to the biblical word describing the onslaught — *"hordes"*.

Verse 7 seems to be a touch of irony.

> *"Be thou prepared, and prepare for thyself, thou,*
> *and all thy company that are assembled unto thee,*
> *and be thou a guard unto them."*

"Thou" refers to the invaders. Charles Lee Feinberg, in his commentary on Ezekiel (The Prophecy of Ezekiel The Glory of The Lord, Moody Press, Chicago, 1969, page 221), helps us to understand the irony here when he says "Ezekiel urged Gog (Russia) to be fully prepared for the encounter, and to see to it that all was in readiness as far as his confederates were concerned. He was to be a guard — actually leader and commander — to them all." The irony actually comes from the fact that the invaders can do nothing but go ahead and invade because God has put hooks in their jaws regarding it.

Verses 8-13 give us the when, where, how and why of the invasion.

Verse 8 is the when and where of the invasion.

> *"After many days thou shalt be visited; in the latter years thou shalt come into the land that is brought back from the sword, and is gathered out of many peoples, against mountains of Israel, which have been always waste; but it is brought forth out of the nations, and they shall dwell safely, all of them."*

"*In the latter years*" of the age of Israel is *when* the invasion will take place. Specifically, at the end of *the times of the Gentiles,* during the time of *Jacob's trouble, the seventieth week of Daniel.* These are all designations referring to the seven–year Tribulation period that precedes the 1,000–year reign of Christ on this earth known as the Millennium.

Irresistible hooks, implanted by God, will bring all the invaders into the land of Palestine. The frog-like demons of Revelation 16:13-14 are one of those hooks. The oil, minerals and the warm water seaport are three more - previously mentioned.

The land brought back from the sword will be invaded. Ezekiel calls this piece of real estate the land *"brought back from the sword"* because Israel has had more wars on its soil than any other place on the planet. It means that the land will be restored from the ravages of the sword because of the peace treaty Israel has entered into with the ruler of the Revived Roman Empire, Beast number one of Revelation 13, that end time Roman prince of Daniel 9:26-27.

Israel during "the latter years", according to the Amplified version of the Bible, will be a land "where people are gathered out of many nations upon the mountains of Israel, which had been a continual waste." All Israel will dwell in peace and safety (1 Thessalonians 5:3) in the land, and even *after* the peace treaty of Daniel 9:27 is broken by the abomination of desolation, in the middle of the Tribulation, the ungodly Jews will still dwell safely.

But to escape martyrdom, the Jews who fear God will flee to the mountains of Edom, Moab and Ammon (Jordan country) while the ungodly ones will go along with the worship of the statue of the first Beast of Revelation 13 that will be placed in the temple. See Chapter Four of this book regarding the Olivet Discourse, and specifically Matthew 24:15, as to the details of how all this will play out. Daniel 11:37-39 and Revelation 13:15 of Chapters Five and Two also deal with this.

Verse 9 goes into the how of the invasion.

"Thou shalt ascend and come like a storm; thou shalt be like a cloud to cover the land, thou, and all thy hordes, and many peoples with thee."

Russia and her allies will overwhelm the Israelis with sheer numbers. Even though Israel has one of the best armies in the world today, it is no match for Russia when it comes to numbers, even if it were activated.

The word *"ascend"* like a storm is used because the Bible always refers to Palestine as *up*. People just don't go down to Palestine. That is in keeping with the fact that Palestine is the land of promise and occupies a special, elevated place in the mind of God and in the minds of the Israelites.

Verses 10-12 give us the why of the invasion.

"Thus saith the Lord God: It shall also come to pass that at the same time shall things come into thy mind, and thou shalt think an evil thought; (11) And thou shalt say, I will go up to the land of unwalled villages, I will go to those who are at rest, who dwell safely, all of them dwelling without walls, and having neither bars nor gates, (12) To take a spoil, and to take a prey; to turn thine hand upon the desolate places that are gathered out of the nations, who have gotten cattle and goods, who dwell in the midst of the land."

Verse 10 tells us it is *"an evil thought"* that causes the invasion of Israel to take place. The evil thought is to attack this land that has disarmed itself and is depending on a peace treaty for its safety from attack. The *"unwalled villages...having neither bars nor gates"* is symbolic language indicating that Israel has disarmed.

One of the things that will make Israel eager to disarm is the crushing burden of having to support its military over the years. I don't know the exact figure for today, but in recent years it has amounted to one–half of its total budget.

Another reason for disarming will be the fact that Beasts one and two of Revelation 13 will be Satan's select men, imbued with power from him, and will convince the Israeli people that Beast number one not only has the smarts to keep the rest of the world off the backs of Israel, but also the military might to enforce such a peace treaty.

Right now the West has no such leader with the genius to concoct and enforce such a treaty, or covenant, as Daniel 9:27 and Isaiah 28:18 refer to it. But, as I mentioned in an earlier chapter, Dr. Charles R. Taylor in his book titled, *The Antichrist King — Juan Carlos*, makes a compelling case for just such a man waiting in the wings. With the military might of NATO behind him, he could *"confirm"* or literally *strengthen* an existing covenant which is being put together by Israel and its surrounding Arab neighbors before our very eyes, today.

The world has not seen a man personally indwelt by Satan since Judas Iscariot. Beast number one will be indwelt by Satan during the last half of the Tribulation and will rule the world — including Russia, Israel, Iran and China — with his charm, intellect and power.

It'll take the likes of a genius to convince the Israelis to stop spending their money for defense and to depend on their only apparent friend in all the outside world, the leader of the West, the Mediterranean alliance.

Right now the U.S. is that leader and friend, and as long as we remain *true* friends we'll not only survive as a nation ourselves, but we'll also be blessed as a nation according to **Genesis 12:3**, *"I will bless them that bless thee and I will curse them that curse thee."* That's what God told the world's first Jew - Abram. But the more the U.S. encourages and pressures Israel today to compromise her security by giving up land for peace the less *true* we are becoming as her friend and the more at risk we are of getting God's curse on us.

At the start of the Tribulation, the ruler of the Revived Roman Empire enters into this covenant with Israel as an assumed true friend, but three and one-half years later he shows his true colors and betrays Israel by demanding that all Jews worship him through a statue of himself placed in the temple by the second Beast, the false prophet of Israel, the one who claims to be the Messiah.

Verse 12 gives another reason for the *why* of the invasion: *"to take a spoil and a prey"*. This refers to the *"hooks"* of verse 4. There we saw that it was a warm water port year round with oil, mineral and chemical wealth. Now we can add to those three *the productivity of the Israeli* people which the words here, *"cattle and goods"* refer to. In addition to that, Israel is the gateway to the riches of Africa. Finally, there's the hook that Egypt represents by its invasion of Israel from the south according to Daniel 11:40. Russia cannot stand to be beat out of this *"spoil and a prey"* by the likes of lowly Egypt.

Verse 13 gives us those who question the invasion.

> *"Sheba, and Dedan, and the merchants of Tarshish, with all its young lions, shall say unto thee, Art thou come to take a spoil? Hast thou gathered thy company to take a prey, to carry away silver and gold, to take away cattle and goods, to take a great spoil?"*

We already know who the invaders are, but the who, here in this verse are *the ones who complain about Russia's invasion* of the prize and *"prey"* that Israel is.

"Sheba and Dedan" refer to the land on the southeast coast of the Persian Gulf where present day *Saudi Arabia* is. This means that she will be allied with the West, *then,* just as she is today. She will evidently not be overthrown by leftist revolutionaries or by Islamic fundamentalists as some have speculated should have happened by now.

"Tarshish" is a name which is used to refer to the West, in general. Geographically it is where *Spain* is located.

"With the young lions", as many conservative Bible expositors believe, refers to the allies of the West, which would probably include such nations in the western hemisphere as the United States, Canada and possibly some South American nations like Brazil. These are also the *"clay"* nations in the 10 toes of Daniel 2:33.

The power bloc of the West makes a charge against Russia and her allies in the form of this question: *"Art thou come to take a spoil? Hast thou gathered thy company to take a prey?"*

Spoils of Ezekiel's day were referred to as *"silver"*, *"gold"*, *"cattle"* and *"goods"*. The big reason Russia waits until the last half of the Tribulation to invade Israel is that Russia has never believed it could get away with it enough until Egypt forces its hand into thinking that it is now or never, for as we know from Daniel 11:40, the King of the South *"pushed at him"*, the second Beast, the false prophet, the dictator of Israel, *the Antichrist*. This will cause *"the King of the North to come against him (the Antichrist) like a whirlwind, with chariots, and with horsemen, and with many ships; and he shall enter into the countries, and shall overflow and pass through"* the main highways of Israel and go on into Egypt, just as Chapter Four in this book details in its explanation of **Daniel 11:36-45**. Chapter Four gives another reason Russia thinks it might suddenly be able to get away with it; Headquarters of the West have been shrouded in complete darkness for a brief time by God's fifth bowl of wrath judgment, thus knocking out Russia's communication system.

There may be a lesson in all this for this nuclear threatened world we live in today. A nuclear World War III holocaust *before* Armageddon does not fit in with the existence of viable and powerful nations from the north, east, south and west fully able to mount a military campaign that will be the greatest in human history. A nuclear World War III holocaust prior to Armageddon would render this planet uninhabitable, leaving few, if any, to populate the Millennium immediately following the Tribulation as Scripture says. God will reduce the earth's population by close to one-half in the Tribulation, but it'll either be the result of His own supernatural judgments which are revealed in Chapters Six through Nineteen of the book of Revelation, or by nuclear weapons as Hal Lindsey makes a good case for in his book, *The Final Battle.*

38:14-23 features the destruction of Russia's army.

In verse 14 God chides Russia with sanctified sarcasm.

> *"Therefore, son of man, prophesy and say unto Gog, Thus saith the Lord God: In that day when my people of Israel dwell safely, shalt thou not know it?"*

God wants Russia and the world to *"know"* that He is well aware that Israel will be defenseless because of that peace treaty with the ruler of the Revived Roman Empire. The sarcasm comes from the words *"shalt thou not know it?"* Of course Russia knows Israel is defenseless; plus the fact that Rome has been blacked out by the fifth bowl judgment of Revelation 16 and knows nothing of what is going on with this or any other invasion.

This won't be the first time Russia has been the big bully on the block. It started with Finland, then Lithuania, Esthonia, Latvia, Czechoslovakia, Hungary, Poland, Bulgaria, Albania, Romania, East Germany, Mongolia and most recently Afghanistan.

None of that includes an equally long list of countries Russia has bullied into submission through its satellite or client countries like Cuba and all the revolutionary subversives in the victim countries like Nicaragua.

But isn't it comforting to know that God has said *"Vengeance is mine, I will repay, saith the Lord"*, **Romans 12:19**? God knows of every injustice on the face of this earth and has declared that *He*, not our flawed legal system, will dispense perfect justice one day in His own way.

Verse 15 tells how Russia can't resist her own greed and heads south with her allies.

> *"And thou shalt come from thy place out of the north parts, thou, and many peoples with thee,, all of them riding upon horses, a great company, and a mighty army;"*

As pointed out in verse 4, *"horses"* were Ezekiel's symbolic way of referring to modern, mobile, military forces which he'd never seen before.

When you combine the armies of Russia with all those of its allies, referred to in verses 5 and 6, it will truly be a *"great"* and *"mighty"* army.

Verse 16 tells that through it all God will be sanctified.

> *"And thou shalt come up against my people of Israel, like a cloud to cover the land; it shall be in the latter days, and I will bring thee against my land, that the nations may know me, when I shall be sanctified in thee, O Gog, before their eyes."*

This means that God will be recognized by all the watching world that He is holy. The conscience of a sin–soddened world knows it has violated God's holiness, and the world recognizes this as a just God vindicating His holiness.

But such recognition does not necessarily translate into acceptance, for in Revelation 6:12-17, the sixth seal judgment, all those against God want the rocks of the mountains to fall on them to hide them from His face and His wrath.

Verse 17 describes how the prophets of old spoke of this judgment.

> *"Thus saith the Lord God: Art thou he of whom I have spoken of old by my servants, the prophets of Israel, who prophesied in those days many years that I would bring thee against them?"*

The prophet Joel, for example, prophesied to Israel that in a future day, he called "the day of the Lord", the nations were to *"prepare war"* and *"let all men of war draw near; let them come up; beat your plowshares into swords, and your pruning hooks into spears; ... Let the nations be wakened, and come up to the Valley of Jehoshaphat; for there will I sit to judge all the nations round about."* Then he closed out the passage (3:9-17) by saying, *"So shall ye know that I am the Lord, your God, dwelling in Zion, my holy mountain; then shall Jerusalem be holy, and there shall no strangers pass through her any more."*

The implied answer to God's question in **Ezekiel 38:17**, *"Art thou he of whom I have spoken of old by my servants, the prophets of Israel?"* is *"yes"*!

Verse 18 reveals God's anger over the invasion of Israel.

> *"And it shall come to pass at the same time when Gog shall come against the land of Israel, saith the Lord God, that my fury shall come up in my face."*

This is the picture of *man* when he gets very angry. The red rises from his neck to his face. But since God, who is a spirit, has no neck or face, He uses this vivid anthropomorphism to communicate to man His fury.

And, with His patience finally exhausted by these continuing efforts to exterminate Israel, the Lord will destroy Israel's enemies either by secondary agencies like human armies with their nuclear weapons, or on His own, God will do all that in His great zeal for Israel.

In verses 19-20, God's threefold fury starts off with an earthquake.

> *"For in my jealousy and in the fire of my wrath have I spoken, Surely in that day there shall be a great shaking in the land of Israel, (20) So that the fish of the sea, and the beasts*

*of the field, and all creeping things that creep upon
the earth, and all the men that are upon the face of
the earth, shall shake at my presence, and the
mountains shall be thrown down, and the steep
places shall fall, and every wall shall fall to the
ground."*

This greatest of earthquakes (Revelation 16:18) would seem to
fit the description of the one in the seventh bowl of wrath John
described in **Revelation 16:17-21**. There Jerusalem will be
divided into three parts. Scripture says, *"the cities of the nations
fell ... and every island fled away, and the mountains were not found."*
Revelation 16:19

Verse 21 gives God's second fury — anarchy.

*"And I will call for a sword against him through-
out all my mountains, saith the Lord God; every
man's sword shall be against his brother."*

Anarchy will infect the ranks of the invaders much like it did
when panic hit the Midianites in Gideon's day when they heard
the bone chilling cry in the still of the night, "The sword of the
Lord and Gideon". That struck terror in their hearts, and they
groggily slashed out at the nearest thing to them in the murky light
of those 300 hand lamps that surrounded their camp. But it wasn't
Israelites' flesh their blades sliced through — it was their own.
These latter day bullies will decimate themselves just as those
bullies did three millennia earlier.

Verse 22 says the third fury is death by six natural disasters.

*"And I will enter into judgment against him with
pestilence and with blood; and I will rain upon him,
and upon his hordes, and upon the many peoples
that are with him, an overflowing rain, and great
hailstones, fire, and brimstone."*

All these words in this verse speak of death by the natural disasters of too much rain, great hailstones (Revelation 16:21
measures them at a talent, 120 pounds each) and fire and
brimstone. They are either natural disasters *supernaturally*
induced, or nuclear weapons in the hands of man. It is strictly
judgment in the hands of an angry God here, either way, yet by

natural disaster would be the most convincing that it was God's judgment.

Hal Lindsey makes a fascinating case for nuclear weapons as the cause of the hail, fire and brimstone here, in *The Final Battle*, his recent book. His research led him to the fact that in a thermonuclear test explosion falling chunks of ice dented the armor plating on the upper deck of one of the surviving test ships. The ones falling on men in 38:22 are about 100 pounds each, according to the weight of a talent in Revelation 16:21.

In verse 23, God's purposes are plainly stated and soberly reiterated.

> *"Thus will I magnify myself, and sanctify myself;*
> *and I will be known in the eyes of many nations,*
> *and they shall know that I am the Lord."*

No one will be able to doubt or argue with this awesome display of God's power intended to magnify Him in the eyes of the world.

Ezekiel 39 will supply us with certain details concerning the events of Chapter 38, or we might say Ezekiel switches from the telescopic to the microscopic.

Verse 1 is a repeat of 38:2-3 — sound familiar?

> *"Therefore, thou son of man, prophesy against Gog,*
> *and say, Thus saith the Lord God: Behold, I am*
> *against thee, O Gog, the chief prince of Meshech and*
> *Tubal,"*

This well may be repeated in order to re-establish the context. It identifies the players and places from which they came.

Verse 2 reveals God's intent to bring to judgment those of verse 1.

> *"And I will turn thee back, and leave but the sixth*
> *part of thee, and will cause thee to come up from the*
> *north parts, and will bring thee upon the mountains*
> *of Israel." ("and leave but the sixth part of thee" is*
> *not in the Hebrew text)*

This also is a repeat, but of 38:22 where God spoke of sending six natural disasters on the invaders. It is repeated for perhaps the same reason as in verse 1.

Verses 3-6 describe God's total destruction of Russia's army and its land at that time.

> *"And I will smite thy bow out of thy left hand, and will cause thine arrows to fall out of thy right hand. (4) Thou shalt fall upon the mountains of Israel, thou, and the peoples that are with thee; I will give thee unto the ravenous birds of every sort, and to the beasts of the field to be devoured. (5) Thou shalt fall upon the open field; for I have spoken it, saith the Lord God. (6) And I will send a fire on Magog, and among those who dwell securely in the coastlands; and they shall know that I am the Lord."*

"Bows and arrows", of verse 3, are symbolic of military might. This is where those billions of Russian rubles, poured into the most massive military machine in human history, will end up. The invaders will *"fall (dead) upon the mountains of Israel"*.

Much of the land of Palestine is mountainous, especially around Jerusalem, which a good relief map will show. Russia will have Jerusalem under siege, just as Zechariah 12:2-4, 9 and 14:1-7 reveal. But the Lord Jesus Christ comes back just in time to annihilate the invaders. That is the meaning of *"ravenous birds of every sort, and to the beasts of the beasts of the field"* to devour thee in verse 4.

Both *"birds"* and *"beasts"* of verse 4, are used symbolically of *total destruction and death*. We will see such symbolism in even greater scope and detail in verses 17-20.

That they will fall on *"the open field"* indicates their destruction is widespread since this refers to the plains of Megiddo which take in a total length of about 200 miles. Revelation 14:19-20 gives quite a picture of all that, but to be precise, it gives a description of the carnage of the campaign of Armageddon and does not necessarily focus on just the destruction of the Russian army and its allies.

Verse 6 speaks of judgment on the *land* of Russia itself. *"Fire"*, in this case, could well be like the fire and brimstone God used on the armies of Russia throughout the mountains of Israel in Ezekiel 38:22. Or, it could be like the hail and fire mixed with blood that burns up the third part of the trees and grass in the first trumpet judgment of Revelation 8:7.

But you'd have to say that if the fire turns out to be nuclear weapons, the very thing Russia was trying to hold the *world* hostage to during the cold war, it would be poetic justice. If nuclear weapons, they might well be from the armies of the east or west who have by now entered the fray.

In any case the fire is directed toward the *continent* of Russia even *from coast to coast*. *"Isles"* in some Bibles is best translated *coastlands*. We already know from 38:2 that Magog is the *land* of Russia.

Verse 7 tells us how this judgment relates to God's purpose for Israel.

> *"So will I make my holy name known in the midst of my people, Israel, and I will not let them pollute my holy name any more; and the nations shall know that I am the Lord, the Holy One in Israel."*

God is *glorified* when He delivers those that are His own. When He does it in your own personal life, whether it be *finan - cially*, from an *illness*, or from just a *desperate situation*, it glorifies Him in *your* eyes and in the eyes of *others* who know of it.

God speaks of making His *"holy"* name known in Israel because the blasphemous speech and conduct of godless Russia have been an assault on the holiness of God, and judgment is the way God chooses to vindicate His holiness. Russia has *"polluted God's holy name"* and this will be its reward.

This is **Exodus 20:7** in action, but on a national scale: *"Thou shalt not take the name of the Lord in vain; for the Lord will not hold him guiltless that taketh His name in vain."*

Israel, when it learns of it, will know that a righteous God has vindicated His holiness and so will the nations of the world. This will also be **Romans 12:19** in action: *"Vengeance is mine, I will repay saith the Lord."*

Israel will no longer blaspheme the name of Jesus Christ as it has done for over 1900 years now. God, after He has judged Russia at Armageddon, will put a new heart in the elect of Israel just as Ezekiel 36:26-38 indicates.

The world needs to know that the living and true God is not only the God of Israel, but that He is also the *holy* God of Israel. To emphasize that, He has repeated the fact of His holiness three times in this 39th chapter, twice in verse 7 and once in verse 25.

Today, the *world* doesn't seem to be all that impressed by the holiness of God until a disaster strikes. That's why some call events like these in Ezekiel "disaster evangelism". Some people get so callused to sin that the only way God can penetrate their hearts and get them to see His holiness and hatred of sin in their lives is to *shock* them to their senses through a *disaster* of some kind. He does it in the Tribulation on a vast scale.

And that is something to bear in mind for your own *personal* life. God's patience, He himself admits, is not without limits, and there may come an end to it when He decides it is best to lower the boom and shake you out of the sin in your life that you keep hanging onto, covering up or otherwise refusing to deal with. A disaster, or series of them, could very well be the boom He lowers in your life as a Christian.

But if you are an unbeliever, He may do it to get you to see your need of "knowing" Him. He repeated *that* refrain once in chapter 38 (verse 23) and three times in Chapter 39 (verses 7, 22 and 28). He wants you to *"know"* Him, and He is prepared to even allow disaster in your life if that is what it takes to wake you up.

God would far rather have you suffer through some disasters here in this life and have you end up knowing Him, than to allow you to continue on in your rejection of Him and end up in the disaster of disasters - the lake of fire for all eternity.

But disaster need *not* lurk around the edges of your life. *Deal* with sin in your life if you're already a believer and put God at the *central*, yes, even the *holy* place that belongs to Him in your life.

Or, if you are an unbeliever, get over on God's side of things by putting Him *in* your life. *Receive* Christ as your Savior. *Miss* the eternal disaster that most surely awaits you if you don't (John 3:18, 36).

Verses 8-10 point to the completeness of the destruction of the invaders.

"Behold, it is come, and it is done, saith the Lord God; this is the day of which I have spoken. (9) And they that dwell in the cities of Israel shall go forth, and shall set on fire and burn the weapons, both shields and the bucklers, the bows and the arrows, and the handspikes, and the spears, and they shall burn them with fire seven years, (10) So that they shall take no wood out of the field, neither

> *cut down any out of the forests; for they shall burn*
> *the weapons with fire; and they shall spoil those*
> *that spoil them, and rob those that robbed them,*
> *saith the Lord God."*

Once again we find more symbols of modern weapons — *"shields"* and *"bucklers"* — but these will all be destroyed. The burning of them with fire is best understood as symbolic of their destruction, for fire has long been a symbol of that. But it does not mean that some of the weapons may not be destroyed with literal fire.

Israel will be able to use the spoils of this battle for quite awhile. That's the meaning of *"So that they shall take no wood out of the field"*. Modern armies use great quantities of diesel fuel and gasoline, thus Israel will be able to use these for its own fuel needs. This will be history's last use of the principle "To the victor belong the spoils".

I also believe that *burning them with fire seven years is symbolic.* The number seven has long been known as the number of completion, and in this case it would be used to tell us of the *completion of the destruction* as well as the *vastness* of the forces of the enemy.

But if it should turn out to be literal, then it would necessitate a period of preparation between the Tribulation and the Millennium known as an *intercalation*, or that the clean–up period of seven years will be allowed to extend on into the Millennium itself as a reminder of what happened.

This is truly poetic justice to have the spoilers be spoiled and the robbers be robbed!

Verses 11-16 describe Israel's cleansing of the land.

> *"And it shall come to pass in that day, that I will*
> *give unto Gog a place there of graves in Israel, the*
> *valley of the travelers on the east of the sea; and it*
> *shall stop the noses of the travelers, and there shall*
> *they bury Gog and all his multitude; and they shall*
> *call it the Valley of Hamon-gog. (12) And seven*
> *months shall the house of Israel be burying them, that*
> *they may cleanse the land. (13) Yea, all the people of*
> *the land shall bury them; and it shall be to their*
> *renown on the day that I shall be glorified, saith the*
> *Lord God. (14) And they shall set apart men for the*

> *continual task of passing through the land to bury,*
> *with the help of the travelers, those that remain upon*
> *the face of the land, to cleanse it; after the end of*
> *seven months shall they make their search. (15) And*
> *the travelers that pass through the land, when any*
> *seeth a man's bone, then shall he set up a sign by it,*
> *till the buriers have buried it in the Valley of Hamon-*
> *gog. (16) And also the name of the city shall be*
> *Hamonah. Thus shall they cleanse the land."*

The vastness of the enemy forces was indicated by the *time* it will take to destroy the debris of battle, and now we see the same truth underscored by the amount of time necessary to bury all the slain. The valley of burial will be the valley of Jordan east of the Dead Sea. It will be so clogged with corpses that the way will be impassable for travelers.

Feinberg, on page 230, aptly comments that "Ironically, although they will only intend to pass through in their campaign for plunder, they will find here the place of their undoing. So great will be the carnage that Gog will give his name to the valley, which will receive a new name commemorating God's victory over Israel's adversaries." The *"Valley of Hamon-gog"* means the multitude of Gog.

It may well take a literal seven months to bury these invaders due to the vastness of the carnage. And there will be the need to cleanse the land of these corpses by such a burial party because the Mosaic Law says *"blood defileth the land"*, Numbers 35:33.

The Jews in the Tribulation will be back under the Mosaic Law as a way of life of which the above Scripture is a part. There will be even those who are assigned the task of disposing of any exposed bones that were overlooked. That's how thoroughly they will obey God's Word.

There's no doubt that this awesome scene of judgment will hone to razor-sharp the Israeli's desire to obey God and His Word. But God doesn't prefer our obedience against a backdrop of judgment, or even divine discipline all the time. He'd much rather have us obey because of our *love* for Him, and even because of our *gratitude* for all He's done for us.

Hamonah, the name of the city located at that burial site, means *multitude* and will be a memorial to remind everyone of the multitudes in the invasion.

When a nation, or an alliance of nations, goes up against the will of God or the people of God, no amount of numbers will insure its success. For example, the Assyrians of Hezekiah's day thought they could intimidate the people of God and insult the God of those people, and this same King of Kings and Lord of Lord's (Revelation 19:16) slew 185,000 of those Assyrian soldiers early one morning without any outside help whatsoever (Isaiah 37:36).

Is it any wonder, with a God like that as your Savior, that you can at all times say with the writer to the Hebrews, *"The Lord is my helper, and I will not fear what man shall do unto me."* **Hebrews 13:5.**

Verses 17-20 give us a buzzard's-eye view of the slaughter.

> *"And, thou son of man, thus saith the Lord God: Speak unto every feathered fowl, and to every beast of the field, Assemble yourselves, and come; gather yourselves on every side to my sacrifice that I do sacrifice for you, even a great sacrifice upon the mountains of Israel, that ye may eat flesh, and drink blood. (18) Ye shall eat the flesh of the mighty, and drink the blood of the princes of the earth, of rams, of lambs, and of goats, of bullocks, all of them fatlings of Bashan. (19) And ye shall eat fat till ye be full, and drink blood till ye be drunk, of my sacrifice which I have sacrificed for you. (20) Thus ye shall be filled at my table with horses and chariots, with mighty men, and with all men of war, saith the Lord God."*

A less facetious and more accurate heading for this section would be, *The Supper of the Great God*, which is exactly what God said about this same scenario in Revelation 19:17. This is not the first and only time God has described such a day of vengeance as *His sacrifice* and even as *"My table"* (verse 20), because it is the Lord who will hold the feast (Isaiah 34:6, Jeremiah 46:10 and Zechariah 1:7-8).

As we mentioned at the very outset of chapter 38, the birds are not literal as 39:20 indicates. Birds can't eat chariots. We don't really have to look for a sudden influx of buzzards in Palestine before Armageddon can take place.

And, as Feinberg observes, on page 231, "The animals mentioned here are figurative of the different ranks of the slain men". The *"rams"*, *"lambs"*, *"goats"* and *"bullocks"* of verse 18 all very well may refer to the gradation of ranks John made when he described the same scene in Revelation 19:17-18. Verse 18 mentions the flesh of kings, captains and mighty men.

God's ultimate purpose is the focus of verses 21-29.

Verses 21-24 state how Israel and the nations will see God's purpose.

> *"And I will set my glory among the nations, and all the nations shall see my judgment that I have executed, and my hand that I have laid upon them. (22) So the house of Israel shall know that I am the Lord, their God, from that day and forward. (23) And the nations shall know that the house of Israel went into captivity for their iniquity; because they trespassed against me, therefore hid I my face from them, and gave them into the hand of their enemies; so fell they all by the sword. (24) According to their uncleanness and according to their transgressions have I done unto them, and hidden my face from them."*

The whole world will see it when God decimates the invaders from the north on the mountains of Israel, and those allied with her, even as implied in Ezekiel 38:21-23, whether He does it Himself or through the nuclear weapons of others.

Feinberg, on page 231, expresses how the world will see God's purpose when he says, "If the people of Israel could discern the working of God among the nations, then it is equally true that the nations of earth could learn the character and will of God from His relationships with His chosen people. Both Israel and the nations of the world are an object lesson for the other. Both display to the other the infinite holiness and love of the universal God. The withdrawal of God's favor from Israel, far from being a result of any caprice, was occasioned by its people's unrepenting opposition to the will of their God."

Holiness is displayed when God vindicates it by punishing Russia at Armageddon for violating His holiness through Russia's relentless persecution of His chosen people.

And *"the nations"* saw a display of God's holiness every time Israel suffered captivity and defeat due to God's divine discipline for violating His holiness when Israelites disobeyed His law.

Thus, *they'll* realize that Israel's failures weren't because of any flaw in God, but because of Israel's sins. **Isaiah (59:2)** summed up Israel's main problem like this, *"But your iniquities have separated between you and your God, and your sins have hidden his face from you, that he will not hear."*

Verses 25-29 reveal that after the defeat of the invaders, Israel will be completely returned and restored.

> *"Therefore, thus saith the Lord God: Now will I bring again the captivity of Jacob, and have mercy upon the whole house of Israel, and will be jealous for my holy name, (26) After they have borne their shame, and all their trespasses by which they have trespassed against me, when they dwelt safely in their land, and none made them afraid. (27) When I have brought them again from the peoples, and gathered them out of their enemies' lands, and am sanctified in them in the sight of many nations, (28) Then shall they know that I am the Lord, their God, who caused them to be led into captivity among the nations; but I have gathered them unto their own land, and have left none of them any more there. (29) Neither will I hide my face any more from them; for I have poured out my Spirit upon the house of Israel, saith the Lord God."*

God will *"bring again the captivity of Jacob"*, or Israel, to an end. He did so in the 70 years captivity in Babylon and now in this captivity under the same times of the Gentiles, from Nebuchadnezzar to the second coming of Christ, He'll do it again.

His mercy to the *"whole house of Israel"*, His elect in Israel (Romans 9:6), will be shown by the dramatic deliverance He brings to His elect. For the exciting details of that deliverance, a look at Zechariah 12:1-14 and 14:1-15 would be a sobering, but rewarding experience. It would also reveal how *zealous* (*"jealous"*) God is for His holy name.

Verse 26 speaks of the *"shame"* Israelites bore when dwelling in their land when *"none made them afraid"*. Their shame was in placing their trust, for peace and safety in the land of Israel, in a mere man — the ruler of the Revived Roman Empire — and not in the almighty God of Israel.

But it is not until they are *"brought again from the peoples and gathered out of their enemies' lands"* and delivered from their captivity — the diaspora — that God will be *"sanctified in them in the sight of many nations"* (verse 27).

Only *"then shall they know"*, as well as many nations, that the Lord is their God (verse 28). He's the one who caused them to be scattered out in the world after the temple was destroyed in 70 AD. It was caused by a judicial blindness (Romans 11:25) imposed by God, and as part of the curse, God said they'd suffer for their disobedience and rejection of Him (Deuteronomy 28-30).

But God did promise to gather them all back into the land and pour out His Spirit upon them (verse 29), even as stated in 36:26-38: believing Israelites, God's elect of Israel, will get new hearts, a new spirit, a heart of flesh to replace their stony, hard hearts and the Holy Spirit within them to enable them to live for God in obedience, and their land, crops and cities will flourish, for now they'll be *"As the holy flock, as the flock of Jerusalem in her solemn feasts ... and they shall know that I am the Lord"* (**Ezekiel 36:38**). Further details of all this are supplied by Joel 2:28-29 and Zechariah 12:10.

Since God in these two chapters - Ezekiel 38 and 39 — is obviously concerned about the bottom line of being glorified, how does that affect you and me who have trusted in Christ as our Savior? Am I bringing glory to God by the way I'm living my life? Am I growing in my knowledge of Him and making continuing progress in putting Him first in my life so that I'm able to obey Him with increasing regularity and faithfulness?

Those are the kinds of questions that test whether we Christians are in step with God's true purpose of bringing glory to His name. The shorter Westminister confession of faith puts it like this: "The chief end of man is to glorify God and to enjoy Him forever."

How about it, are you also *enjoying* God? The answer to that is determined by your answer to the first part — am I *glorifying* God?

The prophetic Scriptures, Peter tells us (2 Peter 3:11), are to be a purifying hope and are to incite the Christian to godly living at all times and especially as we see the day of the Lord approaching.

For those who are not Christians because you have never received Christ as your Savior, the question for you from all of this should be, "Do I really want to continue leaving such a glorious God out of my life, a God who will *not be denied* the glory due His name, a God who will *vindicate* His holiness by punishing sinners like me who *violate* His holiness?

Receive Christ right now by believing that He died for you and for your sins: *"But as many as received Him to them gave He the authority to become the children of God, even to them that believe on His name"* (**John 1:12**).

Chapter Seven

The fourth major player in the Tribulation is the most important one - the winner- the Lord Jesus Christ, God of Israel, King of Kings and Lord of Lords (**Revelation 19:16**).

Here, we will see Christ in His role as Israel's great deliverer as He comes back at His second advent just in the nick of time to rescue the Jews in Jerusalem who are surrounded on all sides—besieged with their backs to the wall - in faith, awaiting His return as their *only* hope. And at His return He not only delivers His own, but single–handedly destroys the armies of the world who have converged on Israel to capture it and take their spoil, but in the end unite to fight Him - their common enemy.

Thus, He ends the Tribulation with the world's armies destroyed, the times of the Gentiles terminated, every city leveled and only His elect ones alive to go on into the Millennium to a refurbished planet — totally cleaned up and renovated — under ideal conditions with Him reigning as a benevolent dictator for 1,000 years of bliss, prosperity unparalleled and world peace that only the Prince of Peace can bring.

Zechariah, Chapter 12:1-9

Verses 1-3 speak of the siege of Jerusalem in the Great Tribulation.

"The burden of the word of the Lord for Israel, saith the Lord, who stretcheth forth the heavens, and layeth the foundation of the earth, and formeth the spirit of man within him. (2) Behold, I will make Jerusalem a cup of trembling unto all the peoples round about, when they shall be in the siege both against Judah and against Jerusalem. (3) And in that day will I make Jerusalem a burdensome stone for all peoples; all that burden them-selves with it shall be cut in pieces, though all the nations of the earth be gathered together against it."

Verse 1 gives us a statement as to the creative power of Jesus Christ much the same as we find in **Colossians 1:16-17** where it says, "For by him were all things created, that are in heaven, and that are in earth, visible and invisible, whether they be thrones or dominions, or principalities, or powers — all things were created by him, and for him; (17) And he is before all things, and by him all things consist." This is mentioned in order to assure the Jews of His ability to deliver, as He'll promise in the verses to follow.

The *"burden"* is God's announcement of a stunning judgment on all who besiege *"Judah and Jerusalem"*. The picture, as verse 2 paints it, is of a drinking goblet filled with believers (in Judah and Jerusalem) and those besieging them are from the armies of the north, south, east and west, for they are like a drunk too wobbly to hold the goblet. This phrase, *"cup of trembling"*, is commonly used by the prophets to refer to future judgments.

The *"burdensome stone"* that God will make of Jerusalem symbolizes that which cannot be lifted or removed. It tells us that all these armies will not be able to conquer Jerusalem. All who try will be *"cut to pieces"*, which symbolizes their own destruction in *"that day"* at the end of the Tribulation when this battle takes place.

Verse 4 describes how the Lord fights for Jerusalem.

"In that day, saith the Lord, I will smite every horse with terror, and his rider with madness; and I will open mine eyes upon the house of Judah, and will smite every horse of the peoples with blindness."

"Every horse" is the ancient prophet's way of describing mobile infantry and mechanized forces that will be deployed against the Jews in Jerusalem in the Great Tribulation. He didn't know the name of a tank or Bradley-type infantry carrier.

These types of forces depend on speed, firepower and fear to immobilize the enemy even to the freezing of the finger on the trigger. But the Lord has His own brand of fear by which He seeks to neutralize these mechanized forces. He does it with *"terror"*, *"madness"* and *"blindness"*. The blindness well might be the result of the supernatural darkness that comes with the second advent of Christ, Isaiah 5:30, 13:9-10 and 60:2; Ezekiel 32:7-8; Joel 2:10-11 and 3:15; Amos 5:18; Matthew 24:29; Luke 21:25-27 and Revelation 6:12.

The *"terror"* and *"madness"* should remind us of the time Gideon terrorized the Midianites in the blackness of the night by suddenly surrounding them with blazing torches mingled with the bloodcurdling battle cry of "the sword of the Lord and Gideon", at the sound of 300 trumpets, Judges 7:20. This caused chaotic anarchy to sweep the ranks of the Midianites where every man's sword was set against his fellow soldier, and the ones who didn't flee were slaughtered by each other. The Lord will use a similar kind of terror against Russia and its allies to finish them off in the Great Tribulation in their invasion of Israel, **Ezekiel 38:21**: *"every man's sword shall be against his brother."*

Verse 5 indicates the faith of the people and their leader.

"And the governors of Judah shall say in their heart, the inhabitants of Jerusalem shall be my strength in the Lord of hosts, their God."

The leaders of Judah were saying to themselves *"The inhabitants of Jerusalem are my strength because the Lord of hosts is their God."* The people, by their faith in God for their deliverance, inspired the leaders. As go the people, so go the leaders. No nation is any stronger than the people's faith in the living and true God not only to deliver them when necessary, but to strengthen and guide in the everyday life and times of the people, as well. In this case they were strengthened to the point where they rose up and fought back as 14:4 indicates.

Verses 6-9 give us the Lord's deliverance because of their faith.

> *"In that day will I make the governors of Judah like an hearth of fire among the wood, and like a torch of fire in a sheaf; and they shall devour all the peoples round about, on the right hand and on the left; and Jerusalem shall be inhabited again in her own place, even in Jerusalem. (7) The Lord also shall save the tents of Judah first, that the glory of the house of David and the glory of the inhabitants of Jerusalem do not magnify themselves against Judah. (8) In that day shall the Lord defend the inhabitants of Jerusalem; and he that is feeble among them at that day shall be like David; and the house of David shall be like God, like the angel of the Lord before them. (9) And it shall come to pass, in that day, that I will seek to destroy all the nations that come against Jerusalem."*

The leaders of the Jews (verse 6), once inspired by the faith of the people in their God, now, in turn, inspire the people *"like a torch of fire among the wood ... and in a sheaf"* of dry grain. This will enable the people to rise up and successfully fight back as the Lord orchestrates their deliverance and victory. In fact, they'll have their victory *"right"* and *"left"* and Jerusalem will be inhabited again in her place as Jerusalem. As a result, the people will peacefully be able to resume their normal lives in Jerusalem.

Verse 7 speaks of *the tents of Judah being saved first.* Merrill F. Unger in his commentary on Zechariah (Unger's Bible Commentary on Zechariah, Zondervan, Grand Rapids, page 212) explains this as follows: "The picture is of the people outside the city walls who do not enjoy the protection or the prestige of the dwellers in the royal metropolis and capital. Because they are more defenseless and exposed, bivouacking in the open country, they shall enjoy God's supernatural interposition *first*, not only as needing it first in point of time since they would be attacked before the city was, but because they needed it first in order that the influential house of David and the proud dwellers of the capital city might not be exalted over them as humble country people... The Lord will manifest Himself in such deliverance as will honor faith, unite His people and cause them mutually to make their boast *wholly* in the Lord, instead of partially in themselves."

In that day (of the Lord) He *"defends the inhabitants of Jerusalem"* so that those who are *"feeble"* and staggering with weakness and fear *"shall be like David"* (verse 8), a mighty and victorious warrior. Centuries later Christians will be commanded in **Ephesians 6:12** to *"be strong in the Lord and in the power of his might."* They can be because Jesus Christ, the head of the Church, is the same One who is also the God of Israel and *"the angel of the Lord"* infinitely able to deliver then as well now.

And when He does defend and deliver in that future day to give Israel its longed for Millennial Kingdom, *"the house of David shall be like God"* in the sense that God will have manifested Himself to mankind not only as "King of Kings and Lord of Lords" (Revelation 19:16), but as David's greater Son.

The Lord, in verse 9, like a heat *"seeking"* missile, attacks all the armies of the nations from the north, south, east and west to utterly destroy them for coming against Jerusalem in their siege and assault. He will thus magnify Himself and sanctify Himself, and He will be known in the eyes of many nations, and they shall know that He is the Lord, Ezekiel 38:23.

Zechariah, Chapter 14:1-7

This chapter continues to give us more details in our exposé of the fourth major player in the Tribulation. We will continue to focus here on the siege of Jerusalem and the Lord's last minute deliverance of His chosen people by His triumphant return to this earth.

Verse 1 tells us of the spoil Israel is to all nations, especially to Russia.

> *"Behold, the day of the Lord cometh, and thy spoil shall be divided in the midst of thee."*

"Thy spoil", as we saw from Ezekiel 38:12, for Russia, will be a warm water port year round, oil, minerals, chemical wealth, the productivity of Israel's people and a gateway to the riches of Africa. Israel will be a spoil to others, as well.

This spoil will be *"divided in the midst of thee"* (Israel) by the invasion and plunder of Israel as set forth in Ezekiel 38 and 39.

Verse 2 indicates the ravages of people and property.

> *"For I will gather all nations against Jerusalem to battle; and the city shall be taken, and the house rifled, and the women*

> *ravished; and half of the city shall go forth into cap -*
> *tivity, and the residue of the people shall not be cut off*
> *from the city.* "

"All nations" will be gathered by God *"against Jerusalem to battle"*. God will use the "hooks" of *"spoils"* mentioned in verse 1 to gather them together to battle. He will also use *"demons working miracles, that go forth unto the kings of the earth and of the whole world, to gather them to the battle of that great day of God Almighty,"* just as **Revelation 16:14** says. The demons would seem to be God's instruments, or even agents, to administer this final roundup.

Half of the city will be captured, the houses looted, the women raped, and the rest of them made prisoners of war in the captured part of the city.

But there will be a remnant (*"residue"*) of the people who will not be defeated (*"cut off"*), but will fight on just as 12:5 and 6 indicate.

Verse 3 describes the slaughter by the Lord at His coming.

> *"Then shall the Lord go forth, and fight against*
> *those nations, as when he fought in the day of*
> *battle."*

"The Lord is a man of war", just as **Exodus 15:3** says. He fought for the children of Israel at the Red Sea where there was a great slaughter of Egyptian soldiers, but that wasn't the only slaughter *"in the day of battle"*. He conducted slaughters of the enemy in His victory at Gibeon (Joshua 10:14), Canaan (Joshua 23:3) and the defeat of Sisera (Judges 4:15). But, perhaps, one of the most dramatic of His slaughters was that of 185,000 Assyrian soldiers early one morning when He smote their camp as they besieged Jerusalem under King Hezekiah, Isaiah 33:36.

No doubt the greatest of His slaughters will be in the final battle of Armageddon when in the 200–mile valley of Megiddo, the blood will be so deep that the New Testament prophet, the apostle John, described its depth as being up to the horses' bridles (Revelation 14:20). That is an awesome amount of blood and slaughter, yet that is the way the Lord, warrior par excellence that He is, fights in order to win.

"Man of war" the Lord might be, yet no one can fault His *patience* before He lowers the boom in judgment. He waited 400

years before judging Canaan, and in the Tribulation there will be many opportunities for disaster evangelism — those eleventh hour reprieves whereby a person who is facing death and eternity through some kind of disaster can avert *eternal* disaster by turning to Christ in faith by trusting in Him as Savior.

Verse 4 reveals Christ's visible return and how He will make an escape route for His remnant.

> *"And his feet shall stand in that day upon the Mount of Olives, which is before Jerusalem on the east, and the Mount of Olives shall cleave in its midst toward the east and toward the west, and there shall be a very great valley; and half of the mountain shall remove toward the north, and half of it toward the south."*

Christ will come back to this earth by planting His feet down on the Mount of Olives, the same spot from which He ascended to heaven and left this earth (**Acts 1:11**). He will evidently be welcomed there by the 144,000 at that time and place (Revelation 14:1).

There is alleged to be a big earthquake fault line at that very spot, and He evidently uses it to *"cleave"* in the midst of it in such a way as to make *"a very great valley"* toward the east and the west in which *"half of the mountain shall remove toward the north, and half of it toward the south."* **Zechariah 14:4** This will be *how* He makes the escape route.

This earthquake would seem to be directly related to the one in the seventh bowl judgment of **Revelation 16:18-19** in which Jerusalem will be *"divided into three parts, and the cities of the nations fell"*. This will no doubt be the worst earthquake in world history for it'll also be worldwide.

Here is the way Merrill F. Unger, in his Commentary on Zechariah, sees Jerusalem after the quake. *"The city, then the capitol of the entire earth, will be situated eminently, the very large valley receding all around it, making it the conspicuous object of admiration, as the city of the great King. The whole land shall be turned into a plain from Geba to Rimmon. But Jerusalem shall remain aloft upon its site (Zechariah 14:10)."* Unger's Bible Commentary on Zechariah, Zondervan, Grand Rapids, MI, 1963, page 247.

Verses 5-7 describe the flight through " the valley of the mountains".

> *"And ye shall flee to the valley of the mountains;*
> *for the valley of the mountains shall reach to Azel;*
> *yea, ye shall flee, as ye fled from before the*
> *earthquake in the days of Uzziah, king of Judah;*
> *and the Lord, my God, shall come, and all the saints*
> *with thee. (6) And it shall come to pass, in that*
> *day, that the light shall not be clear nor dark. (7)*
> *But it shall be one day which shall be known to the*
> *Lord, not day, nor night; but it shall come to pass*
> *that at evening time, it shall be light. "*

Usually the word *"flight"* before an enemy connotes thoughts of people desperately and disorderly fleeing in panic, but due to the supernatural character of the earthquake, it is far more likely that it'll be an amazing and orderly withdrawal. Ours is a God of order (1 Corinthians 14:40). He will be protecting them, and they'll know it — thus, no reason to panic, for He will come *"and all the saints with thee"*. Many other Scriptures refer to His coming back with His saints as we have previously listed, 1 Thessalonians 3:13 and Jude 1:14, notably.

This *"one day which shall be known to the Lord"* is quite unique even as Unger says, page 252, "unparalleled in the annals of human history." Much of what was said in Chapter Four on the Olivet Discourse of Matthew 24:29 can be offered to explain the uniqueness of its being neither day nor night.

That *"it shall be light"* at evening time no doubt refers to that phase of His second coming where *"every eye shall see him, and they who pierced him; and all kindreds of the earth shall wail because of him"* (**Revelation 1:7**). The world's worst nightmare has ended and the dawn of a new Millennium with this first *"light"* of Christ's Millennial Kingdom — that 1,000–year reign of the Prince of Peace, Benevolent Dictator, Lord of Lords and King of Kings.

Jesus Christ is the preeminent One in all of history, and, as such, it is quintessentially fitting that we conclude this book as well as this chapter on the fourth major player in the Tribulation, with the exaltation of Him given in **Philippians 2:9-11,**

> *"Wherefore, God also hath highly exalted him, and given him a name which is above every name, (10) That at the name of Jesus every knee should bow, of things in heaven, and things in earth, and things under the earth, (11) And that every tongue should confess that Jesus Christ is Lord, to the glory of God, the Father."*

This passage is one of several that supports the various reasons Scripture gives for studying prophecy. **Revelation 19:10** says, *"The testimony of Jesus is the spirit of prophecy"*, which means the aim or purpose of prophecy to bring people up to speed as to the Person of Jesus Christ. Still other reasons are that it encourages godliness, holy living (2Peter 3:11) and is a purifying hope (1John 3:3).

Who better to crown as Lord of your life and when better than now?

Bibliography

1. Lindsey, Hal, *There's a New World Coming.* (Vision House, Santa Ana, 1973).
2. Lindsey, Hal, *The Final Battle.* (Western Front, Ltd., Palos Verdes, 1995).
3. Feinberg,Charles Lee, *The Prophecy of Ezekiel The Glory of The Lord.* (Moody Press, Chicago, 1969).
4. Taylor, Charles R., *The Antichrist King - Juan Carlos.*
5. Unger, Merrill F., *Unger's Bible Commentary on Zechariah.* (Zondervan, Grand Rapids, MI, 1963)
6. Vine,W.E., *Expository Dictionary of New Testament Words.*